Entertaining
with Eggs

Entertaining with Eggs

Compiled by
The Canadian
Egg Marketing Agency

PaperJacks LTD.

Markham, Ontario, Canada

AN ORIGINAL CANADIAN

PaperJacks

One of a series of Canadian books
first published by PaperJacks Ltd.

ENTERTAINING WITH EGGS

PaperJacks edition published in July, 1981

ISBN 0-7701-0204-2

CONTENTS

FOREWORD

We have attempted in this book to transform the inexpensive and nutritious but humble egg into over 150 extraordinary dishes for your dining pleasure.

The recipes have been divided into four entertainment occasions — brunch, dinner, after the theatre and dessert. This is intended only as a guide as many are suitable for a variety of occasions.

A section on sauces and drinks, as well as detailed instructions on the basic preparation of omelettes, crêpes, soufflés and poached eggs have been included so that even the novice cook can be assured the gourmet touch.

Many of the recipes can be made ahead of time, either held or frozen and simply popped in the oven for finishing. We hope you will take the opportunity to make ENTERTAINING WITH EGGS a pleasure for you and your guests.

Canadian Egg Marketing Agency

BASICS

SOUFFLÉS

A soufflé is a delicate, puffy dish that can either be an elegant main course or a showy dessert. Soufflés are combinations of a thick sauce, a finely chopped filling and eggs. The yolks and filling are added to the sauce which is then folded into stiffly beaten egg whites. As the air trapped in the mixture expands during baking, the soufflé rises.

A soufflé dish should be of ovenproof glass or pottery and should have straight sides. Because the soufflé should be served directly from the oven to the table, consider a dish that is attractive, as well as practical. Three or four-egg soufflés should be made in a 1½ quart (1.5 L) dish; six-egg soufflés should be made in a 2-quart (2 L) soufflé dish. Some recipes call for an ungreased dish so that as the soufflé rises, it can cling to the sides of the dish. In other recipes, the nature of the ingredients requires a greased dish or a greased dish sprinkled with flour, bread crumbs, Parmesan cheese, or sugar to make it less slippery.

The secret to a successful soufflé is producing a stable egg white foam. Always use a glass or metal mixing bowl, as plastic is porous and may absorb oils. Separate eggs carefully so that no egg yolk slips in with the whites. The fat contained in egg yolks will interfere with the foam formation.

Egg whites should be at room temperature before beating. Beat the egg whites by hand with a large light balloon whisk, using an up and over motion to incorporate as much air as possible. The whites at the stiff peak stage must still be glossy, smooth and moist in appearance but may slip slightly if the bowl is tipped. Air cells should be very small and the peaks should be soft enough so that only the tips fall over when the beater is withdrawn from the bowl. If the egg whites are overbeaten, they will appear dull or flaky. Use a large metal spoon or rubber spatula to fold egg whites into soufflé mixture.

Specific soufflé recipes can be found by consulting the List of Recipes.

OMELETTES

The first step in making a perfect omelette is selecting the right pan. An omelette pan should be thick, slope-sided and of the right size to hold a reasonable number of eggs: a pan with a 7-inch (17.8 cm) base, for instance, will take 3 to 4 eggs. When buying such a pan, choose either thick aluminum or iron. Season the pan by washing it well, and then covering the bottom with salad oil and leaving it for at least 12 hours. Pour off the oil and wipe the pan thoroughly. After this preliminary washing, the pan should not be washed again. Simply scour with salt and wipe off with a paper towel after each use. This treatment helps to maintain an absolutely smooth and slightly greasy surface which prevents the omelette from sticking. If the pan is used for other purposes, for instance, for frying bacon or fish, the surface may have to be scoured to remove burnt particles, and any consequent roughness of the surface is detrimental to perfect omelette making. If, by some chance, an omelette pan is misused and must be washed, dry it well, polish it with a clean cloth dipped in coarse salt or with very fine wire wool and oil it again.

It is inadvisable to make omelettes too big, certainly

not with more than 6 eggs, and preferably 4 at a time, because an omelette larger than this is difficult to cook to perfection. A pan with a base of 7 inches (17.8 cm) in diameter will serve for 3 to 4 eggs, and one of 9 inches (23 cm) will take 6. Omelettes may be cooked in butter. They take various flavours, filling and forms. Sometimes the additional ingredient is added to the egg mixture, sometimes it is used as a filling.

An omelette should not be overcooked; the word "baveuse" is sometimes used to indicate the degree of semi-liquidity. This obviously must be adjusted to suit individual taste, and an omelette may even be cooked so as to be firm throughout, though this idea would shock many a good cook. For those who like a really firm omelette it is probably better to adopt the method for omelette soufflés, which is usually considered suitable only for sweet omelettes, but is often pleasing in savory form to children and to those who find eggs in a liquid state unpleasant.

There are two basic types of omelettes — the plain or French one and the puffy one with a soufflé-like texture. The difference between the two is determined by the method of preparation and cooking. The egg yolks and whites for French omelettes are beaten together and the omelette is cooked over direct heat. When making puffy omelettes, the yolks and whites are beaten separately, cooked over direct heat until browned on the underside, then baked until set.

Be sure to use water, not milk, in omelette egg mixtures. The water turns to steam, producing a light airy omelette. Milk is best for creamy scrambled eggs.

Count on serving 2 eggs per person. The eggs are beaten lightly with a fork, just enough to mix whites and yolks well without making them foamy. Add 2 tbsp. (30 mL) of water, seasoning and, if herbs are to be used, add them at this stage. Heat pan to a point where butter smokes slightly as soon as it is put in; the principle is to use high heat for a short cooking time. When the butter begins to foam, the eggs are poured in. It is from this point that the beginner may need help, and while nothing is as good as visual demonstration, the following will perhaps be better than nothing.

As soon as the eggs are poured in, begin to shake the pan and to stir slowly with the back of a fork rather as if you were stroking the mixture, scraping up large creamy flakes. Pause for a second or two to let cooking proceed; tilt the pan a little away from you and begin to fold the edge well over. As you do this, some of the liquid will escape from the middle of the omelette and come into contact with the hot base of the pan. Set the pan flat again, and when you judge that the omelette has begun to set, lightly draw aside, add any filling called for, tilt the pan away from you, and fold the omelette over quickly. The omelette is now a half-moon in the pan. To turn it out, have a hot dish in your right hand; change the position of your left hand so that it is underneath the handle of the pan, which enables you to tilt the pan well and slip the omelette over to the dish. The whole operation should be quick, taking no more than 2 to 3 minutes. This type of omelette is often referred to as a French omelette.

Specific omelette recipes can be found by consulting the List of Recipes.

CRÊPES

A crêpe is a thin, tender pancake. Unlike pancakes which are served on their own with syrup, the crêpe acts as an envelope and can be filled with anything from eggs, fish and fruit to meats, poultry and vegetables.

The pan, as with omelettes, is most important. A special slope-sided crêpe pan is desirable but any small, 6-10 inch (15-25 cm), seasoned pan will do. Season according to instructions given for omelette pan.

On medium-high heat, heat seasoned pan until just hot enough to sizzle a drop of water. Brush lightly with melted butter. For each crêpe, pour in just enough batter to cover bottom of pan, tipping and tilting pan quickly to move batter over bottom. Smaller pans will take about 2 to 3 tablespoons (30-45 mL) batter, larger pans about ¼ cup (60 mL). Pour off any excess batter. If crêpe has holes, add just a drop or two of batter to patch. Cook until lightly browned on bottom and dry on top. Remove from pan, if desired, turn and brown other side. If your pan doesn't have a non-stick finish you may need to brush it with melted butter after every 2 or 3 crêpes.

Crêpes may be stored in the refrigerator, or in freezer for later use.

To refrigerate crêpes for a day or two, place a sheet of foil, waxed paper or plastic wrap between each crêpe. Cover tightly with plastic wrap or foil or seal in a plastic bag. Store flat.

To freeze crêpes, layer with waxed paper, foil or plastic wrap, as above. Put stack of crêpes on paper plate, in pie plate, deep dinner plate, or round freezer container to protect them. (Crêpes become brittle when frozen and could break.) Cover tightly with plastic wrap or seal in a heavy-duty plastic bag or freezer container. Store flat in your freezer. Crêpes will keep for several weeks.

POACHED EGGS

For poached eggs with a compact oval shape, start with the freshest eggs available. Poach eggs in water that is barely simmering, not boiling. This produces a more tender egg and prevents the white from being disturbed as the egg cooks. Keep eggs from sticking to the bottom of the pan by having water deep enough to cover eggs. The bottom of the pan may also be oiled before water is added.

Adding vinegar to the poaching liquid is unnecessary. The acidity of the vinegar does hasten coagulation or setting of the egg white, but also adds an undesirable flavour. If the water is allowed to boil, even vinegar won't help keep the white together.

To poach eggs, bring water to the boiling point. Use enough water to cover the eggs. Salt or herbs may be added to water for flavour. Reduce heat to simmer; bubbles should not break surface. Break each egg into saucer and slip carefully into water. Cook 3 to 5 minutes depending on firmness desired. Remove eggs from water with slotted spoon. Drain well.

For hard-cooked eggs, poach eggs as usual until yolks are firm, about 15 minutes. Drain and chop to use in recipes calling for chopped eggs.

For semi-poached, use an egg poaching pan or set well-buttered custard cups in one inch of hot water in shallow pan with a tight-fitting lid. Break an egg into each cup. Cover and cook to desired degree.

Eggs may be poached ahead of time and held for up to 2 days. Prepare as directed above, but undercook slightly so that yolks remain runny when reheated. Transfer immediately to pan of cold water, deep enough to cover eggs. Refrigerate. To reheat, dip eggs briefly in hot water for 20 to 30 seconds. Drain and serve.

BRUNCH

MAKE-AHEAD STRATA

8 slices white bread, with crusts removed
slices of Canadian back bacon or ham
slices of sharp Cheddar cheese
3 eggs
¼ tsp. (1 mL) salt
¼ tsp. (1 mL) pepper
½ tsp. (2 mL) dry mustard
¼ cup (65 mL) cup onion and green pepper,
finely chopped
1 tsp. (1 mL) Worchestershire sauce
1¼ cup (315 mL) *whole* milk
dash Tabasco
¼ cup (65 mL) butter
seasoned bread crumbs, crushed

Preheat oven to 350°F. (180°C).

Line bottom of an 8″ x 8″ (20 cm x 20 cm) buttered glass baking dish with 4 slices of bread. Cover with thinly sliced back bacon. Lay slices of Cheddar cheese on top of bacon and cover with remaining bread slices.

In a bowl, beat eggs, salt and pepper. To the egg mixture add dry mustard, onion, green pepper, Worcestershire sauce, milk and Tabasco. Pour over the sandwiches, cover and refrigerate overnight.

In the morning, melt ¼ cup (65 mL) of butter. Drizzle over top. Cover with seasoned bread crumbs. Bake, uncovered, 1 hour. Let sit 10 minutes before serving. Serve with fresh fruit and hot cinnamon rolls.

Makes 4 servings.

OLD COUNTRY STYLE EGGS

5 eggs
2 cups (500 mL) beef stock
3 large tomatoes
¼ cup (65 mL) butter
1 cup (250 mL) finely diced ham
1 cup (250 mL) finely diced pork OR
   ½ lb. (250 mg) cooked minced pork
½ cup (125 mL) finely diced onions
¼ cup (65 mL) all-purpose flour
   Salt and pepper for seasoning

Preheat oven to 350°F. (180°C).

Pour beef stock into a small heavy saucepan and simmer until reduced by half. Blanch the tomatoes and scoop out all the seeds. Chop the tomato pulp coarsely. Melt the butter in a heavy saucepan, add the pork, ham and onions. Cook over low heat, stirring constantly until browned. Combine enough of the stock with the flour to make a smooth thin paste, then stir the paste into the ham mixture. Add the seasonings and simmer until thickened and heated through, stirring frequently. Pour into greased casserole, spreading the mixture evenly. Break eggs carefully into casserole, spacing them decoratively and sprinkle lightly with salt. Bake, covered, for about 20 minutes or until eggs are set. Garnish the border with a ring of freshly chopped parsley. Excellent for brunch or dinner.

Makes 4 servings.

HAM AND EGGS "SEVENTY-FIVE"

2 eggs
1 cup (250 mL) milk
1 cup (250 mL) flour, sifted
1 tsp. (5 mL) baking powder
   salt and pepper to taste
⅓ cup (80 mL) butter, melted
2 slices ham, cut into six
4 hard-cooked eggs, sliced then quartered
1 cup (250 mL) cheese sauce (see page 176)

Preheat oven to 450°F. (230°C).
Heat greased casserole in oven.
Mix all ingredients except ham and hard-cooked eggs into a smooth batter. Place ham and eggs into casserole, and pour batter over. Cook for 5 minutes then reduce heat to 350°F. (180°C) for 25 minutes.
Makes 4 servings.

QUICHE LORRAINE

1 9-in. (23 cm) uncooked pie shell
1 tsp. (5 mL) butter
3 slices peameal or back bacon, ¼" thick, diced
1 medium-size onion, finely chopped
½ cup (125 mL) Swiss cheese, grated
4 eggs, slightly beaten
1 cup (250 mL) milk
1 cup (250 mL) heavy (whipping) cream
   pinch of grated nutmeg
½ tsp. (2 mL) salt
¼ tsp. (1 mL) pepper

Preheat oven to 450°F. (230°C).

In a small heavy saucepan, heat butter. Add bacon and cook for 5 minutes or until golden brown. Remove bacon and set aside. Add onions to pan and cook for 5 minutes. Remove onions and set aside.

Cover bottom of pie shell with bacon, onions and ¼ cup (65 mL) grated cheese. In a mixing bowl, combine remaining cheese, eggs, milk, cream, nutmeg, salt and pepper. Mix well. Pour over bacon mixture. Bake for 15 minutes. Reduce heat to 350°F. (180°C) and continue baking for 15 minutes longer, or until custard is well set. Serve hot.

Makes 4 to 6 servings.

QUICHE ROQUEFORT

1 9-in. (23 cm) pie shell
¼ cup (65 mL) crumbled Roquefort cheese
5 eggs, lightly beaten
1 cup (250 mL) milk
1 cup (250 mL) cream
¼ cup (65 mL) sour cream
½ tsp. (2 mL) salt
¼ tsp. (1 mL) pepper
¼ tsp. (1 mL) grated nutmeg

Preheat oven to 450°F. (230°C).

Partially bake pie shell for 5 minutes. Sprinkle the bottom of shell with crumbled cheese. Combine the eggs, milk, cream, sour cream, salt, pepper and nutmeg and pour over cheese.

Bake for 15 minutes at 450°F. (230°C). Reduce heat to 350°F. (180°C) and continue baking for 10 minutes or until custard is set or until knife inserted near the centre comes out clean.

Makes 4 to 6 servings.

LEEK AND HAM QUICHE

1 9-in. (23 cm) pie shell
4 eggs
2 cups (500 mL) milk or light cream
1 tbsp. (15 mL) flour
½ tsp. (2 mL) salt
dash pepper
⅛ tsp. (0.5 mL) nutmeg
1 tbsp. (15 mL) butter
1 medium leek, thinly sliced
3 thin slices cooked ham, diced
¼ cup (65 mL) grated Gruyère cheese

Preheat oven to 400°F. (200°C).

Partially bake pie shell on lowest rack in oven for 8 minutes. Remove from oven and reduce heat to 350°F. (180°C).

Beat together eggs, milk, flour, salt, pepper and nutmeg.

Melt butter in frying pan over moderate heat. Sauté sliced leek until tender. Add ham and cook for 1 minute. Combine with egg mixture and pour into pie shell. Sprinkle with cheese and bake at 350°F. (180°C) for 35 to 40 minutes or until a knife inserted near the centre comes out clean.

Makes 5 to 6 servings.

BROCCOLI PIE

- 1 9-in. (23 cm) uncooked pie shell
- 1 large onion
- ½ cup (125 mL) mushrooms, sliced
- ½ tsp. (2 mL) oregano
- ¾ tsp. (3 mL) salt
- ¼ tsp. (1 mL) pepper
- 4 tbsp. (60 mL) butter
- 4 oz. (112 g) cream cheese
- ½ cup (125 mL) grated Parmesan cheese
- 1 cup (250 mL) milk, scalded
- 3 eggs
- 1 cup (250 mL) cooked broccoli, chopped
- ½ cup (125 mL) soft bread crumbs

Preheat oven to 425°F. (220°C).

Sauté chopped onion, sliced mushrooms and seasonings in butter until cooked. Mash cream cheese with Parmesan cheese and slowly add scalded milk. Blend in beaten eggs, broccoli, bread crumbs and seasoned vegetables. Spoon filling into an unbaked pie shell and bake for 30 minutes or until filling is set.

Alternate idea: Bacon which has been cooked crisp and crumbled may be sprinkled over top of pie before baking. Tomato slices make a nice garnish as well.

Makes 1 9-in. (23 cm) quiche.

ITALIAN EGG PIE

- 1 9-in. (23 cm) pie shell, plain pastry
- 6 eggs
- ¼ cup (65 mL) milk
- 1 6-7 oz. (168-196 g) can tuna, flaked OR
  1 cup (250 mL) cooked fish, flaked
- ½ lb. (250 g) Mozzarella cheese, grated
- ¼ tsp. (1 mL) salt
- ¼ tsp. (1 mL) ground pepper
- ½ tsp. (2 mL) basil
- ½ tsp. (2 mL) oregano

Preheat oven to 425°F. (220°C).

Beat eggs and milk together until blended. Add remaining ingredients and stir well. Spoon into unbaked crust. Bake until brown, 35 to 40 minutes. Serve hot, cut in wedges.

Makes 6 servings.

FOOLPROOF OMELETTE

  4 eggs, separated
  ¾ cup (175 mL) cottage cheese
  ½ tsp. (2 mL) salt
  ¼ tsp. (1 mL) pepper
  2 tbsp. (30 mL) mild onion or shallots, chopped
  1 tbsp. (15 mL) butter
  2 tbsp. (30 mL) light cooking oil

Beat egg whites until stiff. Place egg yolks, cottage cheese, seasonings, milk and onions in blender. Blend until thick and creamy. Fold in stiffly beaten whites. Heat a large heavy 10-12 in. (25.4-30.4 cm) skillet with oil and butter. Do not let it smoke. Slowly cook the omelette until firm. When omelette is firm, place the pan under the broiler until brown. Additional grated Cheddar cheese may be added before broiling. Fold and serve.

Makes 4 or 5 servings.

SEAFOOD OMELETTE

2 eggs
1 tbsp. (15 mL) light cream
2 oz. (56 g) crab or lobster, diced
3 shrimps, peeled and cut
1 tsp. (5 mL) onions
1 tbsp. (15 mL) dry white wine
2 tbsp. (30 mL) of butter
salt, lemon juice
parsley

Melt 1 tbsp. (15 mL) butter in a frying pan, sauté the onions, shrimps and crab, add a dash of salt and a few drops of lemon juice, add white wine, cover and simmer for 1 minute.

Beat eggs and cream with a fork until blended. Prepare omelette in a second frying pan. When set, fill with crab mixture. Fold, slide onto serving plate and garnish with parsley.

Makes 1 omelette.

OMELETTE VERONIQUE

¼ cup (65 mL) cooked chicken, diced
¼ cup (65 mL) seedless green grapes, halved
⅓ cup (80 mL) undiluted cream of celery soup
2 eggs
2 tbsp. (30 mL) water
  salt and pepper to taste

Combine chicken, grapes and soup; heat until bubbly.

Meanwhile, beat together 2 eggs, 2 tbsp. (30 mL) water and salt and pepper to taste. Heat pan until hot enough to sizzle a drop of water. Place a pat of butter in pan rotating the pan continuously so that the butter does not burn. Quickly pour egg mixture into pan. Once the outer edges of the omelette begin to set, quickly draw them toward the centre of the pan using a spatula. Tilt and rotate the pan enough to allow any uncooked egg to flow into the empty spaces. Direct the handle of the pan toward you and fill one side of the omelette with chicken mixture and fold out onto serving plate. Garnish with additional grapes.

Makes 1 serving.

DELUXE VEGETARIAN OMELETTE

¼ cup (65 mL) Italian salad dressing or clear
   French salad dressing
½ cup (125 mL) shredded carrots
¼ cup (65 mL) green onions, chopped
½ cup (125 mL) cucumber, peeled, sliced and
   seeded
1 tomato, peeled, seeded, chopped
8 eggs
¼ cup (65 mL) milk
1 tsp. (5 mL) salt
¼ tsp. (1 mL) pepper
4 tbsp. (60 mL) butter
1 cup (250 mL) alfalfa sprouts
   plain yoghurt
   snipped chives

In a small saucepan, combine salad dressing, carrots
and onions. Cook over medium-high heat until tender,
stirring often. Stir in cucumber and tomato. Keep
warm while preparing omelette. In a medium bowl,
combine milk, eggs, salt and pepper. Beat with a fork
until well mixed but not frothy. In an 8-in. (20.5 cm)
omelette pan or skillet, melt 1 tbsp. butter over
medium-high heat. When a drop of water sizzles in
the pan, pour in ¼ of the egg mixture. Cook, gently
lifting edges so uncooked portion flows underneath,
until eggs are set. Spoon about ½ cup (125 mL) of the
vegetable mixture onto the omelette and top with
¼ cup (65 mL) of alfalfa sprouts. Fold omelette and
place on plate. Garnish with a spoonful of yoghurt and
a sprinkling of chives. Repeat with remaining butter,
egg mixture and vegetable mixture to make 3 more
omelettes.

Makes 4 servings.

FRITTATA WITH PROVOLONE AND PARMESAN

6 eggs
½ cup (125 mL) grated Provolone cheese
¼ cup (65 mL) grated Parmesan cheese
1 tbsp. (15 mL) finely-chopped parsley
½ tsp. (2 mL) tarragon
    dash salt
    dash pepper
2 tbsp. (30 mL) butter

Beat eggs and blend in remaining ingredients except butter. Melt 1 tbsp. (15 mL) of butter in frying pan or omelette pan over moderate heat.

Pour in half the egg mixture. When eggs form a layer over the bottom of pan, lift edges of omelette allowing uncooked mixture to flow to bottom of pan. When eggs are set, turn omelette over and keep warm. Cook second omelette using remaining butter and egg mixture. Serve on warm plate.

Makes 2 to 4 servings.

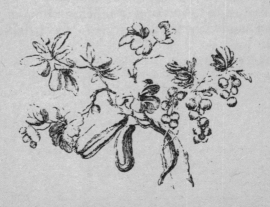

FRITTATA DOMINIQUE

>   1 tbsp. (15 mL) butter
>   ¼ cup (65 mL) green onions, chopped
>   4 medium mushrooms, sliced
>   2 eggs
>   1 oz. (28 g) dry Italian pepperoni, thinly
>   sliced and quartered
>   1 oz. (28 g) mild cheddar cheese, shredded
>   pinch white pepper
>   1 tbsp. (15 mL) milk
>   1½ tbsp. (22 mL) oil
>   3 sautéed button mushrooms

Sauté green onions and mushrooms in butter.

To beaten eggs add the following ingredients: pepper, sautéed onions and mushrooms, pepperoni sausage, shredded cheddar cheese, pepper and milk. Heat oil in an 8-in. (20.5 cm) skillet. Add egg mixture to hot oil in frying pan. Cook eggs on one side, then flip omelette over to finish.

Fold omelette neatly in pan. Place on a plate to serve. Arrange button mushrooms on top of omelette.

This recipe can be used as a luncheon item or as a filling for sandwiches. If preparing for sandwiches, do not fold.

Makes 1 serving.

FRESH WATERCRESS AND
EGG NOUVELLE

   8 eggs
1½ cups (375 mL) blanched and chopped water-
     cress
   3 tsp. (15 mL) olive oil
   ¾ cup (175 mL) onions, sliced
   ½ tsp. (2 mL) salt
   ¼ tsp. (1 mL) freshly ground pepper
   ¼ tsp. (1 mL) fresh basil
   5 tsp. (25 mL) chopped parsley
   ⅓ cup (80 mL) grated Parmesan cheese
   2 tomatoes, thinly sliced
   6 ripe olives, pitted

Preheat oven to 350°F. (180°C).

In a heavy skillet, heat the oil and sauté the sliced
onions. Place the eggs, salt, pepper, basil, chopped
parsley, and blanched and chopped watercress into
bowl, then blend together with a wire whisk.

Add to onions in skillet on top of stove, stirring constantly until eggs begin to set.

Arrange the sliced tomatoes and black olives on top.
Place under broiler to brown, approximately 3 minutes.
Serve immediately.

Makes 6 servings.

BROCCOLI ROULADE

½ cup (125 mL) butter
¾ cup (175 mL) all-purpose flour
1 tsp. (5 mL) dry mustard
1 tsp. (5 mL) salt
¼ tsp. (1 mL) pepper
¼ tsp. (1 mL) nutmeg
4 cups (1 L) milk
6 eggs, separated
1 pkg. frozen chopped broccoli
1 cup (250 mL) cheddar cheese, shredded
   bread crumbs

Preheat oven to 400°F. (200°C).

Generously grease a large jelly-roll pan, line with wax paper, grease again and dust with flour.

Melt butter in large saucepan. Blend in flour, mustard, salt, pepper and nutmeg. Over medium-low heat, stir in milk; cook, stirring constantly, until mixture boils and is thickened. Measure 2 cups (500 mL) of sauce into small saucepan and set aside for making cheese sauce. In a medium bowl, beat egg whites, until stiff and glossy. In another bowl, beat yolks slightly, then slowly beat in remaining hot sauce until thoroughly blended. Fold yolk mixture into beaten egg whites until no streaks of white remain. Spread evenly in prepared pan. Bake in oven about 20 minutes, or until golden and top springs back when pressed with fingertip.

While roulade bakes, cook broccoli, following package directions. Drain well.

Blend cheese into the 2 cups (500 mL) of sauce in saucepan; heat slowly, stirring constantly, until cheese melts and sauce is smooth. Remove roulade from oven and sprinkle with bread crumbs, then cover with a tea towel and turn out of pan. Peel off wax paper. Place cooked broccoli in a single layer on roulade. Spoon on about ⅔ of the hot cheese sauce. Gently roll up lengthwise, using the tea towel to help you. Transfer to serving platter and serve with remaining cheese sauce.

Makes 6 servings.

See insert for a photograph of this dish.

APPLE CREPES WITH ROQUEFORT CHEESE

2 lbs. (910 g) cooking apples
2 tbsp. (30 mL) butter
1 tbsp. (15 mL) sugar
¼ cup (65 mL) butter
4 oz. (112 g) Roquefort cheese
4 oz. (112 g) cream cheese
2 tbsp. (30 mL) table cream
12 prepared crêpes
  sour cream

Preheat oven to 400°F. (200°C).

Peel and thinly slice apples and sprinkle with sugar. Sauté in melted butter until browned but not soft.

Cream cheeses with table cream and spread over surface of crêpes. Put 1-2 tbsp. (15-30 mL) of apples on each crêpe and fold into envelopes.

Place in a buttered dish, dot with butter and bake 15 minutes. Serve with sour cream.

Makes 12 crêpes.

BREAD CRUMB PANCAKES

Toast 6 slices of bread at 200°F. (100°C) until browned (about ½ hour). Roll into crumbs. (Leftover crumbs may be stored in your freezer.)

2 cups (500 mL) unsifted flour
1 tsp. (5 mL) baking soda
1 tsp. (5 mL) salt
1 cup (250 mL) toasted bread crumbs
3 eggs
3 cups (750 mL) buttermilk
⅓ cup (80 mL) melted butter

Preheat fry pan or griddle to 375°F. (190°C).

Stir the flour together with the baking soda and salt in a bowl to blend thoroughly. Mix in the fine dry bread crumbs. Add the unbeaten eggs, buttermilk and melted butter; beat lightly until the eggs are combined and the dry ingredients have all been moistened. Spoon onto the hot, lightly greased griddle to make cakes about 4 in. (10 cm) in diameter. These cakes are good served with maple syrup or whipped honey butter, made by beating together 2 cups (500 mL) honey and 1 cup (250 mL) soft butter until fluffy.

Makes about 20 pancakes, enough for 6 to 8 servings.

CORN FRITTERS

2 eggs, separated
1 cup (250 mL) all-purpose flour
1½ tsp. (7 mL) baking powder
1 tsp. (5 mL) salt
¼ cup (65 mL) milk
1 cup (250 mL) canned corn, drained
oil for frying

Mix egg yolks and milk together and blend with flour, baking powder and salt. Beat egg whites until stiff peaks form. Fold corn and egg whites into batter. Using a teaspoon, drop fritters in oil at 375°F. (190°C) or in a well-oiled frying pan. Turn fritters when golden on the bottom and bubbles begin to appear on the top. Continue to cook until golden both sides. Serve with maple syrup.

Makes approximately 2 dozen.

LAYERED SALAD

¼-½ lb. (125-250 g) bacon
4 hard-cooked eggs
1 head iceberg lettuce, shredded
½ head celery, chopped
1 green pepper, chopped
6 shallots
1 cup (250 mL) frozen peas, thawed
1 cup (250 mL) mayonnaise
2 tbsp. (30 mL) vinegar, tarragon cider or malt
2 tbsp. (30 mL) sugar
2-3 tbsp. (30-45 mL) Parmesan or Romano cheese

Cook bacon until crisp. Drain and crumble. In a large glass bowl, place shredded lettuce layer in bottom. Top with a layer of chopped celery, green pepper and shallots. Sprinkle peas on last. Mix together mayonnaise, vinegar and sugar. Pour dressing over salad. Cover with plastic wrap and chill for at least 4 hours.

Before serving, sprinkle salad with cheese, chopped egg and bacon bits. Garnish with cherry tomatoes.

Makes 10 servings.

SAVORY EGGS

1½ tbsp. (22 mL) butter
½ cup (125 mL) finely-chopped onion
1 19 oz. (530 g) can tomatoes
½ tsp. (2mL) basil
¼ tsp. (1 mL) salt
   dash pepper
⅔ cup (160 mL) crumbled blue cheese
6 hard-cooked eggs, quartered or coarsely
   chopped

Melt butter in saucepan over moderate heat. Add onion and cook until tender. Add tomatoes, basil, salt and pepper and cook gently about 30 minutes until sauce has thickened. Remove from heat.

Mix cheese with ½ cup (125 mL) of the hot sauce. Return to pan and blend until cheese is melted. Return to low heat. Add eggs and heat through. Serve hot on toast or toasted English muffins.

Makes 4 servings.

EGGS ORIENTAL

6 eggs
1 tbsp. (15 mL) dry sherry
  pinch of sugar
  salt and pepper to taste
3 green onions
8 oz. (225 g) fresh, frozen or canned shrimp
¼ cup (65 mL) vegetable oil

Beat eggs lightly in a bowl. Add dry sherry, sugar, salt and pepper.

Finely chop green onions. Shell and de-vein shrimps. Heat half the oil in a skillet. Add shrimps and sauté for 2 minutes (only 1 minute if canned). Add green onion and stir for a further one minute. Remove and combine with the eggs. Heat the remaining oil in skillet. Pour in mixture, stirring until eggs set.

Makes 2 servings.

PIPÉRADE

¼ cup (65 mL) butter or 2 tbsp. (30 mL) oil
1 large onion, finely sliced
2 large green peppers, cut in large strips
1 crushed garlic clove
1 16 oz. (450 g) can tomatoes
   dash salt
   dash pepper
6 eggs, slightly beaten
4 slices bacon, cooked

Melt butter or oil in saucepan over moderate heat. Add onions and cook until tender but not brown. Add green pepper and garlic to onions and cook for 5 minutes. Add tomatoes, salt and pepper. Cover and cook for 20 minutes.

Pour eggs into vegetable mixture and stir constantly until eggs are set. Top with bacon and serve on a warmed platter.

Makes 4 servings.

EGG WITH SHRIMP

- 6 hard-cooked eggs
- 3 tbsp. (45 mL) butter
- 3 green onions, finely chopped
- 1 tbsp. (15 mL) parsley, finely chopped
- ½ tsp. (2 mL) tarragon
- 1 cup (250 mL) small shrimp, chopped into small pieces
- 1 tbsp. (15 mL) prepared mild mustard
- ½ cup (125 mL) heavy cream
  pinch salt
  freshly ground black pepper
- 3 tbsp. (45 mL) grated Parmesan cheese
- 1 tsp. (5 mL) additional butter

Chop eggs finely. Sauté onions in hot butter. Add eggs, parsley, tarragon, shrimp, mustard and heavy cream. Season with salt and pepper. Heat mixture for 3 minutes. Place in a buttered baking dish or individual small dishes. Sprinkle with grated cheese, dot with butter and place under a preheated broiler for 3 minutes until bubbling hot and lightly browned. Serve with toast.

Makes 4 servings.

EGGS BENEDICT

½ cup (125 mL) Hollandaise sauce (See page 179)
8 eggs
8 thin slices ham, or peameal bacon
4 English muffins, split

Lightly fry ham or bacon.
Poach eggs.
While eggs are poaching, toast English muffins. To
serve, place English muffin halves on warmed plates.
Top each with ham or bacon and a poached egg. Spoon
Hollandaise sauce over eggs.
Makes 4 to 8 servings.

POACHED EGGS ON MUSHROOMS WITH MORNAY SAUCE

- 1 lb. (500 g) fresh mushrooms, sliced, or 2 8 oz. (225 g) cans
- 2 shallots, chopped
- 2 tbsp. (30 mL) butter
  dash nutmeg
  dash salt
  dash pepper
- 2 tbsp. (30 mL) Parmesan cheese
- 1 tsp. (5 mL) butter
- 4 eggs
  Mornay sauce (see page 179)
  Parmesan cheese

Sauté mushrooms and shallots in 2 tbsp. (30 mL) butter. Season with nutmeg, salt and pepper. Add 2 tbsp. (30 mL) Parmesan cheese and 1 tsp. (15 mL) butter.

Poach eggs. Place mushrooms on warm ovenproof platter. Remove eggs from water, towel dry and arrange on top. Spoon sauce over top of eggs. Sprinkle with Parmesan cheese and brown under broiler. Serve immediately.

Makes 2 servings.

OEUF POCHE AU BEURRE BLANC À L'ESTRAGON

- 2 poached eggs
  salt and pepper
- ½ tsp. (2 mL) green onions
- 1 tbsp. (15 mL) soft butter
- ⅓ cup (80 mL) crabmeat (5½ oz. [155 g] tin), diced
- 1 tbsp. (15 mL) Chablis wine
- 1 tbsp. (15 mL) 35% cream
- 2 pieces cooked, fresh articoke bottoms (½", rim left on)
- ¼ cup (65 mL) Béarnaise sauce (see page 181)
  Duchess potatoes

In a saucepan, melt the butter, add the green onions and sauté until transparent. Add the crabmeat and Chablis. Simmer for 5 minutes. Add the cream and simmer for an additional 3 minutes. Season.

Poach the eggs and heat the artichoke bottoms. In a shirred egg dish, make a border of duchess potatoes and brown under the broiler. Place the artichoke bottoms on the dish, fill with the crabmeat and place the eggs on top.

Cover with Béarnaise sauce. Sauce can be made ahead and warmed when needed.

Makes 2 servings.

DINNER

PACIFIC SHRIMP OR CRAB MEAT FLAN

3	8 oz. (225 g) cans baby shrimp or crab
8-10	slices white bread
8	eggs, beaten
1	quart (1 L) milk
1	tsp. (5 mL) dry mustard
1	tsp. (5 mL) nutmeg
1½	tsp. (7 mL) salt
1½	lb. (750 g) grated Swiss cheese

Preheat oven to 325°F. (160°C).

Line the bottom of a 9 in. x 15 in. (23 x 40 cm) pan with bread slices from which the crusts have been trimmed. Layer alternately with shrimp and cheese.

Blend the eggs, milk and seasoning. Pour over the shrimp and bread mixture. Place in the refrigerator and let stand for two hours. Remove to room temperature 20 to 30 minutes before baking. Bake for 1 hour.

Alaska king crab can be substituted for the shrimp. Makes 10 to 12 servings.

FRIED GOLDEN EGG

½ cup (125 mL) butter
½ cup (125 mL) onions, chopped
¼ cup (65 mL) green pepper, chopped
½ cup (125 mL) sliced mushrooms, canned
1 cup (250 mL) flour
3¼ cups (815 mL) milk
2 tsp. (10 mL) salt
½ tsp. (2 mL) pepper
1½ tsp. (7 mL) Worcestershire sauce
8 hard-cooked eggs, chopped
1½ tsp. (7 mL) chopped parsely
1 egg
1 cup (250 mL) bread crumbs
½ tsp. (2 mL) paprika
Canadian Cheddar Cheese Sauce (recipe follows)

Sauté onions, green pepper and mushrooms in butter until tender but not browned. Stir in ½ cup (125 mL) flour. Gradually add 2½ cups (625 mL) milk and simmer until thickened. Season with ¾ tsp. (3 mL) salt and pepper and add Worcestershire sauce. Stir in hard-cooked eggs and parsley. Pour into greased pan, cover and chill. Form into 12 4 oz. (112 g) servings; the serving shape should resemble an egg. Mix ½ cup (125 mL) flour and ¾ tsp. (3 mL) salt together. Dredge shaped eggs in seasoned flour. Mix uncooked egg, remaining milk and ½ tsp. (2 mL) salt together. Dip shaped eggs into this mixture and roll in bread crumbs mixed with paprika.

Deep fry at 350°F. (180°C) for 2 minutes or until golden brown. Spoon cheese sauce on plate. Place golden eggs over sauce and garnish with parsley.

Makes 12 servings.

CANADIAN CHEDDAR CHEESE SAUCE

¼ cup (65 mL) butter, melted
½ cup (125 mL) flour
2 cups (500 mL) milk
3 egg yolks
½ lb. (250 g) cheddar cheese, grated
1½ tsp. (7 mL) salt
¼ tsp. (1 mL) white pepper
¼ tsp. (1 mL) dry mustard
dash paprika

Mix together butter and flour. Gradually blend in milk and egg yolks and cook until thickened, stirring constantly. Stir in cheese until melted. Simmer 15 minutes. Add seasonings. Serve with Fried Golden Eggs.

GOURMET MEATLOAF

1½ lbs. (750 g) regular ground beef
1 lb. (500 g) ground pork
1 envelope dry onion soup mix
1 medium onion, chopped
1 uncooked egg, slightly beaten
⅓ cup (80 mL) bread crumbs
3 tbsp. (45 mL) parsley
1 tbsp. (15 mL) Worcestershire sauce
¼ tsp. (1 mL) pepper
½ tsp. (2 mL) thyme
⅓ cup (80 mL) ketchup or chili sauce
4 hard-cooked eggs

Preheat oven to 350°F. (180°C).

In a large bowl, combine all ingredients except hard-cooked eggs. Pack about one-third of the mixture in a 9 in. x 5 in. x 3 in. (23 x 13 x 7 cm) loaf pan. Place hard-cooked eggs lengthwise down the centre of loaf. Pack remaining meat mixture around eggs to completely cover.

Bake 1 hour and 15 minutes.

This is excellent served hot or cold.

Makes 8 servings.

See insert for a photograph of this dish.

BAKED EGGS AND ZUCCHINI CANADIENNE

1 lb. (500 g) zucchini
4 tbsp. (65 mL) onion, diced
1 garlic clove, crushed
3 tbsp. (45 mL) butter
6 eggs
1 cup (250 mL) milk
½ cup (125 mL) Parmesan cheese
1 large tomato, peeled, seeded and chopped
    dash oregano
    dash pepper

Preheat oven to 300°F. (150°C).

Wash zucchini, trim ends, and slice ⅛ in. (0.4 cm) thick. Sprinkle with salt and place in colander. Set aside for at least half an hour to allow excess moisture to drain.

Sauté 2 tbsp. (30 mL) onion and garlic in 1 tbsp. (15 mL) butter. Divide zucchini between 4 buttered dishes (individual oven-proof cooking dishes or 1-quart (1 L) casserole dish may be used). Sprinkle with sautéed onions.

Beat eggs. Slowly warm milk. Add to eggs and beat lightly. Pour over zucchini and sprinkle with cheese. Place in a large pan of hot water. (Water should be halfway up the cooking dish[es] used.) Bake 35 minutes or until set.

Sauté remaining onion in butter. Add tomato and seasonings and cook until hot. Garnish baked eggs with tomato sauce and serve immediately.

Makes 4 to 6 servings.

EGGS MOLLET CHASSEUR

1 tbsp. (15 mL) butter
1 tsp. (5 mL) green onion, chopped
3 mushrooms, chopped
¼ cup (65 mL) chicken stock
1 tbsp. (15 mL) sherry
¼ tsp. (1 mL) salt
  pepper and cayenne to taste
4 poached eggs
2 tbsp. (30 mL) cream
1 tbsp. (15 mL) grated Parmesan cheese

Preheat oven to 400°F. (200°C).

Cook and stir butter and onion for 3 minutes. Add chopped mushrooms and cook for 5 minutes. Add stock, sherry, salt, pepper, cayenne and bring to a boil. Simmer 10 minutes. Pour into shallow baking dish. Place poached eggs in baking dish. Sprinkle 2 tbsp. (30 mL) cream, 1 tbsp. (15 mL) grated Parmesan cheese over eggs.

Bake 10 minutes or until cheese melts.

Makes 4 servings.

EGGS AND WILD RICE ORIENTAL

3-4 eggs, beaten
  4 cups (1 L) cooked wild rice, cold
  3 tsp. (15 mL) soya oil (or vegetable oil)
  4 tsp. (20 mL) green onions, chopped
  2 cups (500 mL) Chinese cabbage, thinly
    sliced
  1 tsp. (5 mL) fresh ginger root, finely
    chopped
  ½ lb. (250 g) Chinese roast pork, diced into
    ½ in. (1 cm.) cubes*
  2 tsp. (10 mL) soya sauce
  ½ cup (125 mL) parsley, chopped
    salt and pepper to taste

In a wok or other type of shallow pan, heat oil to smoking point, then add green onions and wild rice. Mix well and cook until heated through. Add thinly sliced Chinese cabbage and stir for approximately 3 minutes.

Add ginger and diced Chinese pork. Season with salt, pepper and soya sauce to taste. Stir well and heat through, then make a hole in the centre. Add the beaten eggs and mix thoroughly with the wild rice. Fry for approximately 3 minutes.

Place in serving dish. Sprinkle with chopped parsley and serve immediately.

Makes 4 to 6 servings.

*Chinese roast pork can be purchased at a Chinese specialty shop, or can be made by brushing the uncooked roast with Hoisin sauce (about 2 tbsp./lb. [30 mL/500 g]) and allowing it to stand, refrigerated, overnight.

TORTE MILANAISE

1 lb. (500 g) puff pastry (homemade or
   purchased)*
1 tbsp. (15 mL) oil
1 tbsp. (15 mL) butter
1 lb. (500 g) fresh spinach, blanched and well
   drained
2 garlic cloves, minced
¼-½ tsp. (1-2 mL) nutmeg
   salt and freshly ground pepper
2 large red peppers, cut into 1 in. (2 cm)
   pieces and blanched
2 open-face omelettes, each with:
   3 eggs, 1 tsp. (5 mL) chopped chives, 1 tsp.
   (5 mL) chopped parsley, ½ tsp. (2 mL)
   chopped fresh tarragon (or ¼ tsp. (1 mL)
   dried), and salt (prepare in 7 in. - 8 in.
   (18-20 cm) skillet or omelette pan)
½ lb. (250 g) Swiss cheese, coarsely grated
½ lb. (250 g) ham, thinly sliced
1 egg, beaten

Preheat oven to 350°F. (180°C).
Lightly grease 8-in. (20 cm) springform pan. Roll out
three-quarters of pastry, ¼ inch thick and line bottom
and sides of pan. Keep remaining pastry refrigerated.
Heat oil and butter in large skillet. Add spinach and
garlic and sauté 2-3 minutes. Season to taste with
nutmeg, salt and pepper. Remove from skillet.
   Add red pepper to skillet and sauté lightly. Remove
from heat and set aside.

Position rack in lower third of oven. Layer ingredients in prepared pan in following order: 1 omelette, ½ the spinach, ½ the cheese, ½ the ham and all the red pepper. Repeat layering in reverse order, using remaining ham, cheese, spinach and omelette.

Roll remaining pastry ¼ in. (0.5 cm) thick. Cut out 8-in. (20 cm) circle. Place over omelette and seal well to pastry lining by pinching with fingers. With tip of knife, draw the number of slices desired directly on pastry, or decorate with scraps of pastry. Brush with beaten eggs. Place pan on baking sheet and bake until golden brown, about 1 hour, 10 minutes. Cool slightly. Release from pan and cut into wedges with sharp, thin knife.

Makes 6 servings.

*Pastry for an 8- or 9-in. (20 or 23 cm) double-crust pie may be substituted for puff pastry.

LASAGNA

Sauce

    2 tbsp. (30 mL) butter
    1 garlic clove, finely chopped
    ½ cup (125 mL) onion, chopped
    2 7 oz. (196 g) cans tomato sauce
    1 1 lb. (500 g) can tomatoes
    1 tbsp. (15 mL) brown sugar
    1½ tsp. (7 mL) basil
    1 tsp. (5 mL) oregano
    1 tsp. (5 mL) salt
    1 bay leaf

Casserole

    ½ lb. (250 g) lasagna noodles
    2 cups (500 mL) creamed cottage cheese
    1 egg, slightly beaten
    ¼ cup (65 mL) parsley, chopped
    1 tsp. (5 mL) salt
    ¼ tsp. (1 mL) pepper
    ½ cup (125 mL) grated Parmesan cheese
    10 hard-cooked eggs, sliced
    12 oz. (336 g) Mozzarella cheese, thinly sliced

Preheat oven to 350°F. (180°C).

To prepare sauce, melt butter in large saucepan. Add garlic and onion; cook until onion is tender, but not brown. Add remaining sauce ingredients and simmer slowly for 30 minutes, stirring occasionally. Remove bay leaf. (Sauce can be cooked in advance and refrigerated.)

To prepare casserole, cook lasagna noodles according to package directions. Rinse with cold water and arrange on waxed paper to prevent noodles from sticking together.

Combine cottage cheese, egg, parsley, salt, pepper and Parmesan cheese. Spread ⅓ of sauce in shallow 11½ in. x 7½ in. x 1½ in. (30 x 20 x 3 cm) baking dish. Arrange in layers, ½ of the lasagna, ½ of the cottage cheese mixture, ½ of the eggs (reserve centre slices for garnish) and ½ of the Mozzarella cheese. Repeat sauce and layers, ending with sauce. Bake for 35 to 40 minutes. Garnish with egg slices and parsley. Let stand 5 minutes before serving.

Makes 8 to 10 servings.

FRESH WATERCRESS & EGGS NOUVEAUX

8 eggs
1½ cups (375 mL) fresh cooked watercress
3 tsp. (15 mL) olive oil
¾ cup (175 mL) sliced onions
½ tsp. (2 mL) salt
¼ tsp. (1 mL) ground fresh pepper
¼ tsp. (1 mL) fresh basil
5 tsp. (25 mL) chopped parsley
⅓ cup (80 mL) grated Parmesan cheese
2 tomatoes, thinly sliced
6 pitted ripe olives

Preheat oven to 350°F. (180°C).

In a heavy 8 in. x 11 in. (20 x 27 cm) skillet, heat the oil and the sliced onions.

Place the eggs, salt, pepper, basil, cooked watercress and parsley into bowl, then blend together with a wire whisk. Pour into skillet with onions, and cook on top of stove, stirring constantly until eggs start to set.

Arrange the sliced tomatoes and black olives decoratively on top. Sprinkle with grated Parmesan.

Place in oven to brown, approximately 3 minutes. Serve immediately in skillet.

Makes 6 servings.

TUNA AND POTATO CASSEROLE

1 lb. (500 g) potatoes (approximately 3),
  cooked and sliced
2 7-oz. (196 g) cans chunk tuna, drained well
6 oz. (168 g) Swiss cheese, shredded
½ cup (125 mL) sliced green onions
4 eggs
2 cups (500 mL) light cream
1 tsp. (5 mL) dill
1 tsp. (5 mL) pepper
½ tsp. (2 mL) salt

Preheat oven to 325°F. (160°C).
Lightly butter a 1¼-quart (1.25 L) shallow casserole.
Arrange potato slices in an even layer on the bottom,
cover with the tuna (flaked with a fork) and sprinkle
half the grated cheese and green onions on top.

Beat the eggs until blended, stir in the cream, dill,
salt and pepper, and pour into the casserole. Sprinkle
the remaining cheese evenly over the top.

Bake for 45 minutes until the centre moves slightly
when tested with a fork. Cooking time varies with the
size of the casserole; begin checking after 35 minutes.
Sprinkle the remaining onions on the centre of the
casserole and serve.

Makes 6 servings.

OEUF EN COCOTTE COQUILLE

Scallop Sauce

- ½ cup (125 mL) white wine
- 1 8 oz. (225 g) pkg. scallops, cut into quarters
- 3 tbsp. (45 mL) butter
- 3 tbsp. (45 mL) minced onion
- 3 tbsp. (45 mL) flour
- ¼ cup (65 mL) light cream
- ¼ tsp. (1 mL) salt
- dash pepper
- ¼ tsp. (1 mL) lemon juice
- 2 egg yolks
- ⅓ cup (80 mL) sliced mushrooms, cooked

Spinach and Eggs

- 2 tbsp. (30 mL) butter
- 1 small onion, finely chopped
- 1 garlic clove, minced
- 1 10 oz. (280 g) fresh spinach (washed, blanched and coarsely chopped)
- salt and pepper
- 8 eggs
- ½ cup (125 mL) light cream

Preheat oven to 350°F. (180°C).

For sauce, heat wine in saucepan. Add scallops and simmer 2 minutes. Drain, reserving liquid. Melt 3 tbsp. (45 mL) butter in saucepan. Add minced onion and cook until tender but not browned. Blend in flour. Gradually stir in liquid from scallops and half of the ¼ cup (65 mL) cream. Add salt, pepper and lemon juice. Mix egg yolks with the remaining cream and add to the hot but not boiling sauce. Heat for 1 minute. Thin with additional wine, if necessary. Stir in scallops and mushrooms. Pour into a 13 in. x 9 in. (33 x 23 cm) casserole dish or 4 individual cocottes (baking dishes).

For spinach, melt 2 tbsp. (30 mL) butter in frying pan. Add chopped onion and cook until tender. Stir in spinach and garlic. Season with salt and pepper.

Spread spinach over scallop sauce. With back of spoon, make 8 hollows in spinach; break an egg into each hollow. Pour ½ cup (125 mL) cream over top. Cover with lid or foil. Place pan of hot water in oven and set cocotte(s) in pan of water. Bake 12-15 minutes or until eggs are set.

Makes 4 to 8 servings.

BAKED CRAB CASSEROLE

8 eggs
2 cups (500 mL) milk
¼ cup (65 mL) flour
2 6 oz. (168 g) cans of crab, drained and flaked
3 tbsp. (45 mL) butter
½ cup (125 mL) onion, chopped
½ cup (125 mL) celery, thinly sliced
2 tbsp. (30 mL) parsley, chopped
½ tsp. (2 mL) salt
¼ tsp. (1 mL) pepper
¼ tsp. (1 mL) thyme
    few drops Tabasco sauce
1 tbsp. (15 mL) lemon juice

Preheat oven to 350°F. (180°C).

Thoroughly beat eggs with milk. Blend in flour; add flaked crab. Sauté onion and celery in butter until tender. Add to mixture along with remaining ingredients; stir.

Place in greased 9 in. x 9 in. (23 x 23 cm) baking dish. Cover with a lid or foil. Bake for 45 minutes, or until firm. Sprinkle with additional chopped parsley. To serve, cut in squares or spoon out.

Makes 6 servings.

CURRIED EGGS AND PINEAPPLE

2 tbsp. (30 mL) oil
1 large onion, chopped
1 apple, chopped (optional)
1 tbsp. (15 mL) flour
1 tbsp. (15 mL) curry powder
1 14 oz. (400 g) can pineapple cubes
   dash salt
¼ cup (65 mL) sultana raisins
1 tbsp. (15 mL) Mango chutney (optional)
1 tbsp. (15 mL) desiccated coconut (optional)
9 hard-cooked eggs
2 cups (500 mL) cooked rice

Heat oil in frying pan and cook onion and apple until tender. Add flour and curry powder. Cook for 3 minutes.

Drain pineapple, reserving juice. Add water to pineapple juice to make 2 cups (500 mL). Add liquid to curry mixture and bring to a boil stirring constantly. Add salt, raisins, chutney and coconut. Simmer 20 minutes.

Cut 8 hard-cooked eggs in half lengthwise and add to curry mixture. Stir in pineapple, setting a few pieces aside for garnish. Continue to cook until heated through.

Place cooked rice on large platter. Arrange eggs down centre of rice and cover with curry sauce. Garnish with pineapple and the remaining hard-cooked egg which has been sliced.

Makes 4 - 5 servings.

EGGS IN JACKETS

  4 large potatoes (for baking)
 10 eggs
  6 large, ripe tomatoes
  2 tbsp. (30 mL) tomato paste
  1 onion, finely chopped
  3 garlic cloves, finely chopped
  2 tbsp. (30 mL) anchovy paste
 20 pitted black olives
 ½ cup (125 mL) soft butter
 ¾ cup (175 mL) table cream
   salt and pepper
   ground nutmeg
   thyme, bay leaf, rosemary (finely ground)
   or 1 tsp. (5 mL) Italian seasoning
   parsley, chopped, and parsley sprigs

Preheat oven to 350°F. (180°C).

Wash and scrub potatoes. Dry well. Coat in melted butter and place in oven. Bake for 1½ hours. Turn occasionally to brown evenly.

Clean and core tomatoes. (Save a few slices for decoration.) Chop finely.

In a saucepan, brown the onion and garlic in a little butter. Add chopped tomatoes and paste. Cook over a low heat until liquid forms. Add the anchovy paste and chopped olives (save a few slices for decoration). Season with salt, pepper, a pinch of thyme, rosemary and finely ground bay leaf, and a dash of nutmeg to taste. Let simmer a few minutes over a low heat. Set aside on simmer while scrambling eggs.

Cut baked potatoes in two lengthwise. Scoop out the
two halves. Keep potatoes warm in oven while scramb-
ing eggs. Fill with a generous coating of tomato sauce.
Stuff with scrambled eggs. Decorate with tomato slice
down the middle, a few olive slices, chopped parsley
and parsley sprigs.

Serve hot.

Makes 4 servings (8 halves).

CHICKEN MARENGO WITH FRENCH FRIED EGGS

3-4 lbs. (1½-2 kg) chicken parts, uncooked
4 cups (1 L) tomato sauce
1 garlic clove, finely chopped
1 medium onion, chopped
½ tsp (2 mL) coarsely ground pepper
1 tsp. (5 mL) salt
2 bay leaves
1 tsp. (5 mL) dried oregano, crumbled
¾ cup (175 mL) raisins
1 tbsp. (15 mL) oil
1 tbsp. (15 mL) vinegar

Preheat oven to 350°F. (180°C).
Combine all ingredients except the chicken in a large casserole with cover. Stir to blend. Add chicken parts and spoon sauce over. Cover and bake 1½ hours or until chicken is tender. Garnish with french fried eggs.

French Fried Eggs

6 eggs
oil

Heat oil in a deep fryer or large pot to 350°F. (180°C). Break eggs into oil. Cook 1 minute. Drain well on paper towels. Season. Serve at once.
Makes 6 servings.

EGGS ARTEMISIA

2 slices ham, diced
2 tbsp. (30 mL) shallots or green onions, diced
3 tbsp. (45 mL) celery hearts, diced
4 eggs
¼ cup (65 mL) water
½ tsp. (2 mL) salt
  dash pepper
¼ tsp. (1 mL) tarragon, crushed
1 tbsp. (15 mL) oil
1 garlic clove, peeled and halved
  soya sauce

Preheat oven to 350°F. (180°C).

Place ham, shallots and celery in medium mixing bowl. Add eggs and beat until mixed. Add water, salt, pepper, tarragon and oil to egg mixture and mix thoroughly.

Rub the inside of 2 small baking dishes no larger than 4 in. (10 cm) square with garlic halves. Pour egg mixture into baking dishes and sprinkle with a few drops of soya sauce. Place the dishes in a pan of hot water. Bake for 20 minutes or until just set. Serve hot or cold.

Makes 2 servings.

EGGS ROYALE

4 cups (1 L) mashed potatoes
9 eggs
1 tbsp. (15 mL) butter
6 tbsp. (90 mL) onion, chopped
6 strips bacon, diced
6 tbsp. (90 mL) tomato (about 1 large), chopped
  salt and pepper to taste
  6 tbsp. (90 mL) cheddar cheese, grated

Preheat oven to 400°F. (200°C).

To prepare Duchess Potatoes, combine potatoes, 1 uncooked egg, butter and salt to taste, mixing until very smooth. Divide potatoes between 4 ovenproof individual serving dishes, piping or spooning them into nests about 4 inches in diameter.

Poach 8 remaining eggs. Meanwhile, sauté onion and bacon together for 3 minutes, then add chopped tomatoes. Adjust seasoning.

Place 2 poached eggs in each potato nest and top with bacon mixture, then grated cheese. Bake until potatoes are lightly browned.

Makes 4 servings.

SOFT-COOKED EGGS, ARMOURY

12 soft-cooked eggs
6 cups (1.5 L) cooked leaf spinach
2 oz. (56 g) butter
½ cup (125 mL) chopped onion
1 garlic clove, finely chopped
salt and pepper to taste
12 artichoke bottoms
24 white asparagus tips
2 cups (500 mL) Hollandaise sauce (See page 175)
4 ripe olives, sliced

Heat butter in a pan until slightly brown. Add onions and garlic, and stir for thirty seconds. Add spinach, salt and pepper.

Warm the artichoke bottoms and asparagus tips in a small amount of their own liquid to which a tablespoon of butter has been added.

Spread the hot spinach on a warmed platter. Press the warmed artichoke bottoms in a circle or any preferred design. Place one warmed egg in each artichoke bottom, then coat with the Hollandaise sauce.

Place two white asparagus tips between each egg (tips all pointed towards the rim of the platter). Place one slice of ripe olive on top of each egg and serve immediately.

Makes 6 servings.

GOLDEN EGGS

- 4 soft-poached eggs
- 3 green onions
- ½ tsp. (2 mL) parsley
- 5 tbsp. (75 mL) butter
- ½ tsp. (2 mL) tarragon
- 1½ cups (375 mL) dry white wine
- 1 cup (250 mL) table cream
- 1½ tbsp. (22 mL) hot mustard
- 1 lb. (500 g) puff pastry shells (obtainable from your grocer)
- salt and pepper

Preheat oven to 400°F. (200°C).

Poach the eggs; set aside.

Brush the pastry shells with egg yolk.

Peel and chop the onions finely. Wash and pat dry. Chop the tarragon and parsley. Cut the butter into small pieces.

Place the chopped onions, half of the tarragon and the white wine in a small saucepan. Let half of the moisture evaporate over medium heat. Add the cream. Again, let the liquid evaporate.

Remove the saucepan from the heat. Add the butter, mustard; season to taste. Beat well with a whisk. Place to one side.

Place the poached eggs in the middle of pastry shells. Pour sauce over. Sprinkle with parsley and remainder of tarragon. Bake for 5 minutes.

Makes 4 servings.

ARTICHOKE SLICES

4 eggs, well beaten
¼ cup (65 mL) seasoned croutons, crumbled
2 12 oz. (340 g) jars marinated artichoke hearts, drained and cut up
1 small onion, sautéed in butter
1 cup (250 mL) medium Cheddar cheese, shredded
salt and pepper

Preheat oven to 350°F. (180°C).
Mix all ingredients and add to well beaten eggs.
Pour into a 9 in. x 9 in. (23 x 23 cm) pan. Bake for 35 minutes.
Can be served immediately or frozen for future use. Serve warm.
Makes 6 servings.

EGGS LISE

2 tbsp. (30 mL) butter
2 tbsp. (30 mL) flour
1 cup (250 mL) milk, scalded
⅓ cup (80 mL) grated old Cheddar cheese
   dash dry mustard
   salt and pepper
3 English muffins, split, buttered and toasted
6 slices turkey roll, ¼ in. (0.5 cm) thick
1 seedless orange, peeled, cut in cross sections
   ⅛ in. (0.25 cm) thick
6 soft poached eggs
2 tbsp. (30 mL) grated orange rind

In a medium saucepan, cook butter and flour over medium heat until well blended. Add milk and blend until smooth. Add cheese and dry mustard. Allow to simmer about 15 minutes. Season to taste. Top with butter or wax paper to prevent a skin forming. Set cheese sauce aside.

Top each English muffin half with slice of turkey roll, an orange slice and a soft poached egg. Ladle ¼ cup (65 mL) of cheese sauce over poached egg and place under broiler until sauce is slightly browned. Garnish with grated orange rind.

Makes 3 servings.

POACHED EGGS BIAROTTE

2 pears, peeled and cored
2 tbsp. (30 mL) butter
3¼ cup (815 mL) dry red wine
   dash of salt, pepper and nutmeg
1 tsp. (5 mL) sugar
2 tbsp. (30 mL) flour ⎫
1 tbsp. (15 mL) butter ⎬ optional
2 large potatoes, peeled
2 tbsp. (30 mL) butter
4 poached eggs
1 cup (250 mL) ham, diced

Cut pears in fine julienne* strips.

Melt butter in saucepan. Add pears, sauté until tender. Add wine, salt, pepper, nutmeg and sugar. Cover and simmer 40 minutes. If necessary, thicken sauce by mixing flour and butter until pea-size balls are formed. Add to wine and pear sauce and bring to a boil. Cut potatoes in fine julienne* strips or grate. Melt butter in frying pan. Add potatoes and cook until brown on all sides. Place in mounds on 4 serving plates, dividing evenly.

Place an egg on each mound of potatoes. Cover with sauce and sprinkle with ham.

Makes 4 servings.

*Julienne cut indicates thin, long strips.

DESSERTS

COLD CHOCOLATE MOUSSE

4 eggs, separated
¾ cup (175 mL) semi-sweet chocolate chips
5 tbsp. (75 mL) boiling water or coffee
2 tsp. (10 mL) vanilla

In a small bowl, beat egg whites until stiff but not dry. Place chocolate chips in blender container; whirl until powdery. Add boiling liquid and blend until smooth. Add egg yolks and vanilla. Blend for 30 seconds. Scrape mixture down from sides of container and blend for 30 seconds more.

Pour chocolate mixture over egg whites. Fold gently and thoroughly. Spoon into individual dishes. Refrigerate until well-chilled (at least 1 hour). Garnish with whipped cream, if desired.

Makes 4 servings.

See insert for a photograph of this dish.

MOCHA SWIRL CHEESECAKE

Crust

> 1 cup (250 mL) graham cracker crumbs
> ¼ cup (65 mL) melted butter
> ½ cup (125 mL) chopped pecans
> ½ tsp. (2 mL) cinnamon

Filling

> 2 cups (500 mL) milk
> 2 envelopes gelatin
> 1 tbsp. (15 mL) instant coffee
> 4 eggs, separated
> 2 8 oz. (225 g) pkg. cream cheese
> 1 6 oz. (168 g) pkg. chocolate chips
> ⅓ (80 mL) cup Kahlua (or other coffee liqueur)
> ½ cup (125 mL) sugar
> 5 oz. (140 g) chocolate to decorate - optional

For crust, combine graham cracker crumbs, melted butter, pecans and cinnamon and press onto bottom of 9 in. (23 cm) spring form pan. Chill. For filling, mix gelatin and coffee with 1 cup (250 mL) milk in saucepan. Heat egg yolks with 1 cup (250 mL) milk and stir into gelatin mixture. Stir over low heat until gelatin is dissolved. Remove from heat. Beat cream cheese and ¼ cup (65 mL) sugar until smooth. Gradually beat in gelatin mixture (or blend in food processor). Chill until mixture mounds slightly when dropped from spoon. Meanwhile, melt chocolate chips with ⅓ cup (80 mL) Kahlua. Cool.

Beat egg whites until soft peaks form. Gradually add ¼ cup (65 mL) sugar and beat until stiff.

Fold in gelatin mixture. Combine chocolate with 2 cups (500 mL) gelatin mixture and alternate spoonfuls with the remaining gelatin mixture in the prepared crust. Swirl with a knife to marble, and chill until firm.

To decorate, melt 5 oz. (140 g) of chocolate. Pour the chocolate onto a cookie sheet and spread into a thin layer. Chill for 10 minutes. Using a narrow paint scraper or putty knife, scrape bands of hardened chocolate from the opposite side of the cookie sheet, towards you. The chocolate will form accordion-like pleats when scraped. Place these pleats on the meringue. Continue until top is covered. Refrigerate until ready to serve.

Makes 4 servings.

CHOCOLATE ALMOND TORTE

Base

½ cup (125 mL) slivered almonds
2 tbsp. (30 mL) sugar
1 cup (250 mL) water
½ cup (125 mL) butter, cut into pieces
1 cup (250 mL) flour
4 eggs

Custard

¾ cup (175 mL) sugar
3 tbsp. (45 mL) cornstarch
2½ cups (625 mL) milk
3 eggs
2 tsp. (10 mL) almond extract
6 tbsp. (90 mL) powdered sugar
¼ cup (65 mL) butter, room temperature

Chocolate Glaze

4 ozs. (112 g) chocolate
3 tbsp. (45 mL) butter
2 tbsp. (30 mL) sugar
½ cup (125 mL) whipping cream (garnish)

Preheat oven to 400°F. (200°C).

Mix almonds and sugar; set aside. For base, combine water and butter in medium saucepan and bring to rolling boil. Reduce heat and add flour all at once. Beat until dough forms ball and no longer sticks to sides of pan. Remove from heat and add eggs one at a time, beating until mixture loses its sheen before adding next egg. Lightly grease 3 9-in. (23 cm) cake pans. Divide base evenly among pans, spreading to edges with spatula. Sprinkle with sugar-nut mixture. Bake

15 minutes. Press dough down with spatula. Reduce oven temperature to 375°F. (190°C) and continue baking until dough is lightly browned, about 15 minutes. Turn off heat, open oven door and let pastry stand 10 minutes. Remove from pans and let layers cool completely on wire racks.

Stir sugar and cornstarch together in heavy saucepan. Beat in milk and eggs until thoroughly combined. Bring to boil over medium heat, beating constantly until thickened, about 5 minutes.

Immediately set pan in cold water and stir custard until cool. Add extract. Beat powdered sugar and butter in medium bowl until smooth. Add custard a few tablespoons at a time and beat until thoroughly mixed.

Melt chocolate and butter together over low heat. Working quickly drizzle over each layer of base.

Place one layer, chocolate side up, on platter. Mound half of custard in centre. Add second layer chocolate side up and press lightly to spread custard. Repeat with remaining custard and top layer. Chill. Just before serving, whip cream and pipe-around top and sides of torte. Cut with sawing motion to ensure stability of filling.

Makes 8 servings.

CREAMY MOCHA MOUSSE

4 eggs, separated
4 tbsp. (60 mL) sugar
1 tsp. (5 mL) instant coffee ⎫ OR 3 tbsp.
3 tbsp. (45 mL) hot water ⎬ (45 mL)
⎭ strong coffee

3 oz. semi-sweet chocolate
1¼ oz. (37 mL) coffee liqueur
3 tbsp. (45 mL) heavy cream
1½ cups (375 mL) heavy cream, whipped
    garnish: semi-sweet chocolate

Beat egg yolks until lemon-coloured. Add sugar gradually, beating until fluffy. Blend in coffee and water. In a small pan, stir yolk mixture over low heat until thickened. Let cool.

Melt chocolate in large glass or stainless steel bowl over hot water. Remove from heat. Blend in the yolk mixture, coffee liqueur and 3 tbsp. (45 mL) of whipping cream.

Beat egg whites until stiff but not dry. Fold into cooled chocolate mixture. Fold in whipped cream.

Pour into 8 to 10 sherbert glasses and refrigerate for 2 hours. Garnish with chocolate shavings.

Makes 8 to 10 servings.

POTATO CHOCOLATE TORTE

1½ squares unsweetened chocolate
½ cup (125 mL) butter
1½ cups (375 mL) sugar
2 tbsp. (30 mL) hot water
3 eggs, separated
1½ cups (375 mL) mashed potatoes
1¾ cups (425 mL) flour
1 tbsp. (15 mL) baking powder
¾ cup (175 mL) ground walnuts or hazelnuts
1½ tsp. (7 mL) vanilla

Preheat oven to 350°F. (180°C).

Melt chocolate and set aside. Cream together butter, sugar and water. Beat in egg yolks. Blend in melted chocolate and mashed potatoes and beat until smooth.

Beat egg whites until stiff, and fold into creamed potato mixture. Add flour, baking powder, walnuts and vanilla and stir until evenly mixed.

Pour into a 9 in. (23 cm) springform pan or into a 10 in. (25 cm) tube pan. Bake 45 minutes. Cool. Turn out on a serving dish and ice with your favourite icing.

Makes 6 to 10 servings.

CHOCOLATE MERINGUE DESSERT

Meringue

> 3 egg whites
> ½ tsp. (2 mL) vinegar
> ¼ tsp. (1 mL) cinnamon
> ¼ tsp. (1 mL) salt
> ½ cup (125 mL) sugar

Preheat oven to 275°F. (140°C).

Beat egg whites with vinegar, cinnamon and salt until soft peaks form. Gradually add sugar until stiff peaks form. Cover a greased baking sheet with brown paper or parchment. Make an 8 in. (20 cm) circle and spread meringue, building the sides. Bake for 1 hour. Turn oven off and leave meringue to dry for 2 hours. When cool, peel off paper and fill with Chocolate Mousse.

Chocolate Mousse

> 1 8 oz. (225 g) pkg. semi-sweet chocolate chips
> 3 egg yolks
> ¼ cup (65 mL) water

Melt the chocolate chips in a saucepan over low heat. Drizzle 2 tbsp. (30 mL) of chocolate over meringue. To remaining chocolate add yolks and ¼ cup (65 mL) water. Set aside.

Cinnamon Whipped Cream Layer

   1 cup (250 mL) whipping cream
   ¼ cup (65 mL) sugar
   ¼ tsp. (1 mL) cinnamon

Whip the cream and gently fold in sugar and cinnamon. Spread half the mixture over meringue base.

Gently fold the rest of the whipped cream into chocolate and egg yolk mixture. Spread chocolate mousse over cinnamon whipped cream layer and chill.

Meringue may be decorated with whipped cream and toasted almonds or pecans.

Makes 8 servings.

BAKED CHOCOLATE SOUFFLÉ

   3 tbsp. (45 mL) butter
   3 tbsp. (45 mL) all-purpose flour
1½ cups (375 mL) milk
   7 oz. (196 g) semi-sweet chocolate
   1 tbsp. (15 mL) instant coffee
  ¼ cup (65 mL) water
   8 eggs, separated
     pinch salt
  ¾ cup (180 mL) granulated sugar

Preheat oven to 400°F. (200°C).

Butter a soufflé or shallow pyrex baking dish. The large oval shape is recommended as it guarantees that the centre of the soufflé will cook properly.

Prepare a sauce in a saucepan over medium heat by melting butter and adding flour. Cook for 30 seconds. Remove from heat and whisk in the cold milk all at once. Return pan to heat and bring sauce to simmer, stirring constantly with a whisk.

In the top of a double-boiler, melt the chocolate, add instant coffee and water. Stir until smooth. Add beaten egg yolks and stir until yolks have thickened the chocolate mixture. Add the sauce and blend well. Remove from heat and cover, unless it is to be used immediately. This will hold for 1-2 hours at room temperature. When ready to bake, rewarm sauce (if necessary) over double-boiler before adding to beaten egg whites.

Beat egg whites with a pinch of salt until they form soft peaks. Gradually add the granulated sugar until firm peaks form. Gently fold warm sauce into egg whites. Pour soufflé mixture into buttered baking dish. Bake for 25 to 30 minutes until centre is set. Sprinkle with confectioner's sugar and serve at once, spooning it onto warm plates. Serve with whipped cream or ice cream.

Makes 8 servings.

CHOCOLATE CREME CARAMEL

2 cups (500 mL) sugar
3 whole eggs
5 egg yolks
2 cups (500 mL) partially skimmed chocolate milk
2 cups (500 mL) heavy (whipping) cream
½ tsp. (2 mL) salt
2 tbsp. (30 mL) Kahlua (or other coffee or cocoa-based liqueur)
2 tbsp. (30 mL) instant coffee
¾ cup (175 mL) slivered hazelnuts

Preheat oven to 350°F. (180°C).

In a skillet, melt one cup (250 mL) sugar over medium heat, stirring constantly until sugar melts and turns into a golden brown syrup. Pour into a warmed 8-cup (2 L) mold or individual custard cups. Tip mold back and forth to coat inside completely with the caramel syrup. Allow to cool.

Meanwhile, beat eggs and egg yolks together. Beat in 1 cup (250 mL) of the chocolate milk. Gradually beat in remaining cup (250 mL) of sugar until completely dissolved. Add the rest of the chocolate milk, cream and salt. Mix the Kahlua and instant coffee thoroughly. Blend into the previously caramelized mold(s). Sprinkle slivered hazelnuts evenly on top.

Place in centre of a shallow pan of hot water. Bake in oven. (Individual custard cups about 1 hour; large ring mold 1¼ to 1½ hours, or until a knife inserted in centre comes out clean.)

While hot, invert a serving dish over the baking mold. Reverse quickly and the creme caramel will slip out.

For best flavour and texture refrigerate before serving.

Makes 8 servings.

MERINGUES

4 egg whites
1 cup (250 mL) sugar

Filling

½ cup (125 mL) whipping cream
1 tbsp. (15 mL) chocolate sauce

Preheat oven to 250°F. (120°C).

Grease 3 large cookie sheets with oil, or line with non-stick heavy kitchen parchment.

Beat egg whites until stiff. Continue to beat, adding sugar a little at a time, beating well after each addition until all the sugar has been added. Using two wet spoons, spoon the meringue mixture onto prepared baking trays, or pipe in rosettes using a large star tube.

Sprinkle with sugar and place in oven for 1½ to 2 hours or until dry. Remove from oven and cool on rack.

Whip cream and add the chocolate. Sandwich two meringues together with filling.

Makes 2 dozen meringues.

MERINGUE CAKE

5 egg whites
1½ cup (375 mL) powdered fruit sugar

Preheat oven to 275°F. (140°C).

Cover 3 cookie sheets with brown paper. Beat egg whites until very stiff. Beat in 1 tbsp. (15 mL) of sugar. Fold in the remaining sugar.

Fill a pastry bag and pipe 3 7-in. (18 cm) circles onto the paper. Bake 1 hour and 15 minutes until they are slightly brown and completely dry.

CHOCOLATE MOUSSE

5 oz. (140 g) bittersweet chocolate
½ cup (125 mL) butter
3 eggs, separated
1½ tbsp. (22 mL) sugar

Melt chocolate very slowly. Take off heat and add butter stirring well. When cooled, stir in egg yolks one by one. Beat egg whites until soft. Beat in sugar and continue until they hold stiff peaks. Fold chocolate into egg whites. Chill well.

Place meringue on serving plate. Spread some mousse on meringue, put on another layer of meringue, more mousse and finish with another meringue layer. Coat the sides of cake with the mousse.

MINTED MERINGUE ICE

3½ cups (875 mL) milk
1 cup (250 mL) granulated sugar
1 tsp. (5 mL) peppermint extract
4 egg whites
2 oz. (56 g) semi-sweet chocolate (coarsely chopped)
sprigs of fresh mint

Heat the milk, sugar and peppermint extract, stirring gently until sugar is dissolved then bring to boiling point. Remove from stove to cool.

Pour the cooled milk mixture into a suitable plastic container and place in freezer. Leave until semi-frozen.

Beat the egg whites until stiff but not dry. Break up the semi-frozen ice with a fork, then fold in the beaten egg whites. Return to freezer until frozen. Spoon the minted meringue ice into stemmed glasses, top with chopped chocolate and sprigs of mint.

Makes 6 servings.

FROZEN LEMON CREAM

6 tbsp. (90 mL) butter, melted
2 tsp. (10 mL) lemon peel, grated
⅓ cup (80 mL) lemon juice
1 cup (250 mL) sugar
3 eggs
3 egg whites
1 cup (250 mL) whipping cream

In the top of a double-boiler, blend together butter, grated peel, lemon juice, ¾ cup (175 mL) of sugar and 3 whole eggs. Cook over simmering water, stirring constantly until mixture is thickened. Remove from heat and chill.

Beat egg whites until stiff, then gradually beat in the remaining ¼ cup (65 mL) of sugar until stiff glossy peaks form when the beater is withdrawn. Whip the cream until stiff, stir in the chilled lemon mixture and fold in egg whites. Pour into a plain 6-8 cup (1.5-2 L) mold, cover and freeze for 8 hours or overnight. To unmold, immerse pan in hot water to a level slightly above the frozen mixture for 15 seconds. Hold mold upside down on serving dish and shake firmly to remove. Smooth the sides with a spatula. Freeze for 30 mintues to firm up the exterior. Cut in wedges and serve with berries and more whipped cream if desired.

Makes 8 to 10 servings.

HOLIDAY BOMBÉ

2 pints (1 L) pistachio ice cream
2 pints (1 L) chocolate ice cream or other
favourite flavour

Chill a 2½-quart (2.5 L) bowl. Soften pistachio ice cream slightly. Line bowl with plastic film or foil. With the back of a large spoon press softened ice cream (first layer of bombé) over the interior of the bowl. Return to freezer and freeze until firm. Soften second flavour and repeat pressing ice cream onto pistachio flavour. Return to freezer until firm. Prepare the Coffee Tortoni for the center.

Coffee Tortoni

3 egg whites
2 tbsp. (30 mL) instant coffee
¼ tsp. (1 mL) salt
½ cup (125 mL) sugar
2 tsp. (10 mL) vanilla
¼ cup (65 mL) raisins, chopped
¼ cup (65 mL) mixed candied fruits, chopped
1 tbsp. (15 mL) rum
¾ cup (185 mL) toasted almonds, finely
chopped
2 cups (500 mL) whipping cream

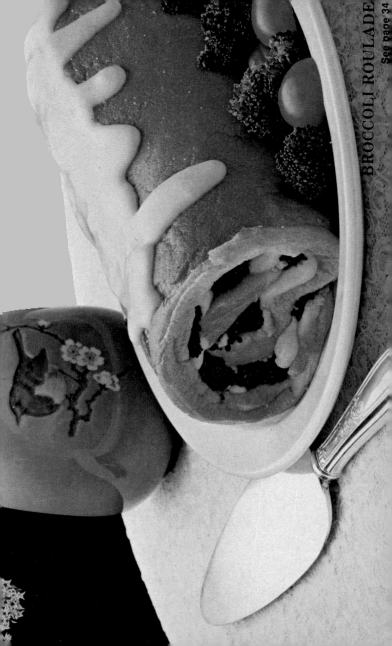

BROCCOLI ROULADE
See page 34

GOURMET MEATLOAF
See page 52

COLD CHOCOLATE MOUSSE

See page 79

ITALIAN EASTER BREAD
See page 134

SHRIMP QUICHE
See page 139

GOLDEN EGG CRÊPES
See page 146

CHEDDAR CHEESE SOUFFLÉ
See page 158

EGGS COMTESSE
See page 165

Mix raisins, fruit and rum. Let stand about 30 minutes. Beat egg whites with coffee and salt. Gradually add ¼ cup (65 mL) sugar. Whip the cream until it forms soft peaks. Add remaining vanilla and ¼ cup (65 mL) sugar. Fold cream into egg whites and add marinated fruit and almonds.

Fill the centre of the bombé with this mixture. (Any remaining filling may be frozen in lined muffin cups. This makes a delicious dessert on its own). Freeze bombé until firm. Turn bombé out on a sheet of foil and decorate with individual meringues and/or whipped cream. Return to freezer. After frozen, wrap well in foil and return to freezer until ready to use. Let soften 30 minutes in the refrigerator before serving. As this recipe serves 18 to 20, it may be easily halved, using a 1¼ quart (1.25 L) mold or bowl to serve 10.

CREAM PUFFS

1 cup (250 mL) boiling water
½ cup (125 mL) butter
¼ tsp. (1 mL) salt
1 cup (250 mL) all-purpose flour
4 eggs

Preheat oven to 425°F. (220°C).

Place water, butter and salt in a saucepan and bring to boil. When butter is melted and mixture is boiling, incorporate flour all at once. Stir rapidly until mixture forms a ball that comes away from the sides of pan. DO NOT OVERCOOK as this will cause the flour and fat to separate.

Remove from heat and add eggs, UNBEATEN, one at a time, mixing well after each addition. A mixer or food processor is ideal for this job as long beating is the secret to a tender puff.

Grease a cookie sheet. Form paste into desired shape, forming dough with the back of a spoon.

1 tbsp. (15 mL) of mixture makes 1 large puff or eclair. 1 tsp. (5 mL) of mixture makes 1 bite size puff.

Eclairs are rectangular shaped puffs 3 in.-4 in. (7-10 cm) long by 1 in. (2 cm) wide, best shaped using a pastry bag.

Baking the puffs: A very hot oven is essential to puff the paste. Bake at 425°F. (220°C) for 30 minutes or until well risen and set. Reduce heat to 325°F. (160°C) for about 10 to 15 minutes or until puffs are dry and golden colour. When baked, place puffs on a wire rack until cool. When shells are cold, fill the puffs with sweetened whipped cream, ice cream or custard. Sprinkle with icing sugar and serve with chocolate or butterscotch sauce or sweetened fruits in season.

Makes 1 dozen eclairs or 7 dozen bite-sized puffs.

French Vanilla Cream Filling

- 1½ cups (375 mL) milk, scalded
- 3 egg yolks
- ⅓ (80 mL) cup sugar
- ¼ cup (65 mL) flour
- 1 tbsp. (15 mL) butter
- ¼ tsp. (1 mL) salt
- 1 tsp. (5 mL) vanilla

Sift sugar, flour and salt and place in top of double-boiler. Add hot scalded milk a little at a time, stirring well after each addition. Cook in double-boiler until thickened, stirring constantly. When thick, cover saucepan and continue to cook for 20 minutes longer. Beat egg yolks slightly and add a little of the hot mixture to them. Mix well and return to double-boiler custard. Cook for an additional 2 minutes. Remove from heat and add butter and vanilla. Cool before filling cream puffs. For a richer custard, cream may be substituted for milk or 1 cup (250 mL) stiffly beaten whipped cream may be folded into cool, cooked custard. Top with chocolate icing or butterscotch cream sauce, or chocolate custard sauce.

For sauce recipes see pages 175-184.

POACHED PEARS WITH CRÈME ANGLAISE

6 pears, slightly underripe
4 cups (1 L) water (or half dry white wine)
2 cups (500 mL) sugar
2 tbsp. (30 mL) fresh lemon juice
1 tsp. (5 mL) lemon rind
1 cinnamon stick
3 whole cloves
  almond slices, toasted

Peel the pears, cut in half lengthwise. Core. Bring water and/or wine, sugar and flavourings to a boil. Add pear halves and poach until tender. Pears will be translucent and easily pierced with a kitchen fork.

With a slotted spoon, remove pears from syrup, place on a tray and sprinkle with toasted almonds. Serve pears on a glass dish and surround with Crème Anglaise. Serve additional sauce separately.

Makes 12 servings.

Crème Anglaise

   2 cups (500 mL) milk
   1 cup (250 mL) whipping cream
   ¾ cup (175 mL) sugar
   8 egg yolks
   2 tsp. (10 mL) vanilla extract
   2 tsp. (10 mL) cornstarch

Combine milk, cream and vanilla extract in a saucepan. Bring just to boil. Remove from heat and let stand 10 minutes to absorb flavour of vanilla. Gradually beat sugar into the egg yolks and continue beating until pale yellow and creamy. Beat in cornstarch. Stir in the warm milk mixture and beat vigorously with a wire whisk to prevent any lumps. Return the mixture to the saucepan and cook over low heat until mixture coats the back of a spoon. This will take about 15 minutes. DO NOT BOIL! Remove from heat and cool, stirring frequently.

Serve warm.

BANANA DAIQUIRI SOUFFLÉ

2 envelopes unflavoured gelatin
1 cup (250 mL) sugar
⅛ tsp. (0.5 mL) salt
5 eggs, separated
1¼ cups (310 mL) water
1 tsp. (5 mL) grated lime rind
1¼ cup (315 mL) lime juice
¼ cup (60 mL) light rum
2 tbsp. (30 mL) banana liqueur (optional)
4 ripe bananas
½ pint (250 mL) whipping cream

Make a 4 in. (10 cm) collar of double thickness waxed paper or foil and place it around the top of a soufflé dish. Tape or clip together so that it fits snugly and extends 3 in. (7 cm) above rim of the dish.

In a small saucepan, combine gelatin, ½ cup (125 mL) sugar and salt. Beat egg yolks and water and stir into gelatin mixture. Stir constantly over low heat until gelatin completely dissolves and mixture thickens slightly, about 5 minutes. Remove from heat and stir in lime rind, lime juice, rum and banana liqueur. Chill, stirring occasionally, until mixture is slightly thickened.

Beat egg whites in large bowl until soft peaks form. Gradually beat in remaining ½ cup (125 mL) sugar, beating until stiff after each addition. Fold in gelatin mixture. Dice and fold in three bananas. Whip and fold in 1 cup of the cream. Turn into prepared 6-cup (1.5 L) soufflé dish. Chill until firm. To serve, remove collar and garnish with remaining whipped cream and sliced banana.

Makes 8 to 10 servings.

Recipe may be halved, using 3 eggs.

BANANA SOUFFLÉ CRÊPES

Crêpes

3 eggs
1 cup (250 mL) milk
2 tbsp. (30 mL) butter, melted
¾ cup (175 mL) flour
1 tbsp. (15 mL) sugar
¼ tsp. (1 mL) salt

Preheat oven to 350°F. (180°C).

Beat together eggs, milk and melted butter. Stir in dry ingredients until smooth. Heat 6-in. (15 cm) skillet; brush with butter. Pour in 2 tbsp. (30 mL) batter, tilting pan to spread. Brown both sides. Repeat with remaining batter.

Makes 8 crêpes.

Filling

4 eggs
4 bananas
¼ cup (65 mL) butter
4 tsp. (20 mL) icing sugar

Separate eggs. Peel and slice bananas in saucepan. Place saucepan over low heat, add butter and stir until mixture becomes fairly dry. Remove from heat. Add yolks to banana mixture. Beat egg whites until stiff. Add sliced bananas.

Divide mixture between 8 crêpes, bake for 5 to 6 minutes. Pour vanilla sauce over crêpes and serve.

For vanilla sauce recipe, see page 183.

Makes 4 servings.

STRAWBERRY BLINTZES

- 1 cup (250 mL) all-purpose flour
- 3 tbsp. (45 mL) sugar
- ¼ tsp. (1 mL) salt
- 5 eggs
- 1⅓ (330 mL) cups milk
- 2 cups (500 mL) strawberry yogurt
- ½ cup (125 mL) strawberry preserves
  - butter
  - powdered sugar

In a medium bowl, mix flour, sugar and salt. In another bowl, mix 3 eggs and milk. Gradually add milk mixture to flour mixture, beating with electric mixer on medium speed until blended. Cover and chill for 2-3 hours.

Using a preheated crêpe pan over medium high heat, brushed with oil, place 2 tbsp. (30 mL) of batter in pan. Cook until browned on bottom. To remove crêpe, loosen edges and gently lift with spatula. Stack crêpes between squares of waxed paper for easy separation.

In a medium bowl, slightly beat two remaining eggs. Stir in yogurt and ½ cup (125 mL) strawberry preserves. Place crêpes browned-side up and spoon about 1½ tbsp. (22 mL) yogurt mixture onto the centre of each crêpe. Fold crêpe over the filling — first the bottom, then the side and finally the top, envelope style.

In a large skillet, melt 2 tbsp. (30 mL) butter. Brown blintzes over medium heat on both sides, adding more butter, if necessary. Sprinkle blintzes with powdered sugar and top with a spoonful of strawberry preserves.

Serve immediately.

Makes 20 blintzes.

THE GOLDEN CUP

6 eggs, separated
¾ cup (175 mL) sugar
    pinch of salt
¼ cup (65 mL) Grand Marnier
½ cup (125 mL) milk
1 lb. (500 g) pkg. frozen whole strawberries
    (unsweetened)

Marinate strawberries in 2 tbsp. (30 mL) Grand Marnier and ¼ cup (65 mL) sugar or substitute 1 pkg. of the sweetened berries and ½ cup (125 mL) milk. Combine egg yolks, salt, ¼ cup (65 mL) sugar, 2 tbsp. (30 mL) Grand Marnier and ½ cup (125 mL) milk and cook in a double-boiler, beating constantly until thick.

Beat egg whites until foamy. Gradually add ¼ cup (65 mL) sugar and beat until stiff peaks form.

Using a large ice cream scoop, drop egg whites into boiling water and poach for 2 minutes turning several times.

Place strawberries in a champagne glass, reserve 6 small ones for garnish. Place poached meringue on top, cover with cooked egg yolk mixture and garnish with one small strawberry.

Can be served warm or cold.

Makes 6 servings.

STRAWBERRY MERINGUE CREAM TORTE

Meringue rounds

>   4 egg whites
>   ¼ tsp. (1 mL) cream of tartar
>   1 cup (250 mL) sugar
>   ¼ tsp. (1 mL) salt

Filling

>   2 cups (500 mL) whipping cream
>   ⅓ cup (80 mL) sugar
>   2 cups (500 mL) fresh strawberries
>   6 ozs. (168 g) semi-sweet chocolate bits
>   3 tbsp. (45 mL) water

Beat 4 egg whites at room temperature with cream of tartar and salt until mixture forms soft peaks. Gradually add sugar and beat until stiff. Draw 3-8 in. (7-20 cm) circles on sheets of brown paper or parchment which have been spread on greased cookie sheets. Spread a thin layer of meringue on each circle — about ¼ in. (0.5 cm) thick. Bake at 250°F. (120°C) for 45 minutes or until dry and lightly colored. Let cool and carefully remove from the paper.

Beat the cream until it holds soft peaks. Beat in sugar and continue to beat until stiff. In the top of a double-boiler, melt the chocolate bits with 3 tbsp. (45 mL) water. Hull, wipe and slice the strawberries, reserving a few nice whole ones for garnish. Put a meringue round on a cake plate and spread with a thin layer of melted chocolate. Cover this layer with a ¾ in. (1.5 cm) layer of whipped cream and top with half of the sliced strawberries. Arrange a second series of layers in the same manner over the first and top with the remaining meringue round. With a metal spatula, spread the remaining whipped cream around the sides of the torte. Decorate with remaining chocolate and strawberries. Chill torte for at least 4 hours.

Alternate: Chocolate Mousse Filling

     5 ozs. (140 g) semi-sweet chocolate
     ½ cup (125 mL) butter
     3 eggs, separated
     1½ tbsp. (22 mL) sugar

Melt chocolate slowly on low heat in a medium size pan. Remove from heat and add butter, stirring well. When mixture is cool, add beaten egg yolks. Beat egg whites until soft peaks form. Add sugar and continue to beat until stiff peaks form. Fold chocolate into egg whites and chill well.

When using the chocolate mousse filling, spread on plain meringue layers followed by more mousse and then meringue. Decorate with whipped cream and strawberries.

Makes 8 servings.

ORANGE POUNDCAKE

    1 cup (250 mL) butter
 2¼ cups (565 mL) sugar
    6 eggs
    3 cups (750 mL) sifted cake flour
    ½ tsp. (2 mL) salt
    ½ tsp. (2 mL) baking soda
    1 cup (250 mL) sour cream
    1 tbsp. (15 mL) grated orange rind
    1 tsp. (5 mL) vanilla

Preheat oven to 350°F. (180°C). Grease the bottom of
a 10-in. (25 cm) tube pan and line with waxed paper or
parchment. Using an electric mixer, beat butter until
soft and fluffy. Add sugar and beat until well blended.
Add eggs, one at a time, beating well after each
addition. Sift the flour with salt and baking soda,
then add alternately with sour cream to butter, sugar
and egg mixture. Stir in orange rind and vanilla.
The batter will be fairly thick. Spoon batter into
prepared cake pan. Bake in centre of oven for 1½ hours
or until a cake tester inserted in centre comes out
clean. Let stand for 5 minutes before pouring hot
orange glaze over the top of the cake. Let cake sit for
1 hour before removing from pan.
    Makes 8 servings.

Orange Glaze

    1 cup (250 mL) orange rind
    ¾ cup (175 mL) sugar
    ¼ cup (65 mL) butter
    1 tbsp. (15 mL) lemon juice

Combine ingredients in a small saucepan. Bring to a

boil. Lower heat and simmer 10 minutes. Pour over the cake while hot.

ORANGE CUSTARDS

  2 oranges
1½ cups (375 mL) milk
  ½ cup (125 mL) whipping cream
  4 eggs
  ¼ cup (65 mL) sugar
  1 tbsp. (15 mL) Grand Marnier
    mint leaves

Preheat oven to 300°F. (150°C).

Peel the skin from one orange into thin strips. Place orange strips in saucepan of boiling water and cook over medium heat for 5 minutes. Remove from heat and run under cold water. Drain and dice finely.

Heat milk and cream until just warm. Beat eggs and sugar together. Blend in warm milk. Strain mixture through fine sieve. Stir in diced orange peel and Grand Marnier. Pour into four lightly buttered custard cups, soufflé molds or ramekins. Set dishes in large pan of water. Water should be halfway up baking dishes. Bake 45 minutes or until custards are set. Remove from hot water, cool and refrigerate.

Peel second orange and cut both oranges into sections. Chill sections in their own juices.

Gently loosen the edges of each custard using a small knife. Invert onto a chilled dessert plate and arrange orange sections in a pinwheel on top. Pour a little orange juice over each custard. Decorate with mint leaf in centre of pinwheel.

Makes 4 servings.

ORANGE CLOUD SOUFFLÉ

1 6 oz. (168 g) tin orange juice concentrate,
   thawed
1 envelope gelatin
½ cup (125 mL) sugar
4 eggs, separated
½ cup (125 mL) rum
1 cup (250 mL) heavy cream, whipped
   dash salt

Lightly beat egg yolks. Soak gelatin in concentrated orange juice for 5 minutes. Add ¼ cup (65 mL) sugar and egg yolks. Mix well. Simmer mixture, stirring constantly until thickened. Add rum and chill until thickened. Fold in whipped cream. Beat egg whites with salt until soft peaks form. Add remaining ¼ cup (65 mL) sugar and continue to beat until stiff peaks form. Fold egg whites into orange gelatin mixture. Pour Orange Cloud into a soufflé dish or elegant glass bowl which has been lined with lady fingers. Refrigerate for 2 hours.

Garnish with whipped cream.

Makes 6 servings.

LADY FINGERS

¼ cup (65 mL) granulated sugar
3 eggs, separated
1 tbsp. (15 mL) vanilla extract
    pinch salt
⅛ tsp. (0.5 mL) cream of tartar
1 tbsp. (15 mL) granulated sugar
⅔ cup (160 mL) sifted cake flour
1½ cups (375 mL) powdered fruit sugar

Preheat oven to 300°F. (150°C).

Lightly grease two baking sheets with butter, dusting with flour and tapping off excess flour. In a mixing bowl, beat the sugar and egg yolks. Add vanilla and continue to beat until mixture is thick.

In separate bowl beat egg whites with salt and cream of tartar until soft peaks form. Sprinkle in 1 tbsp. (15 mL) sugar and continue to beat until stiff peaks form. Gently fold egg whites and sifted flour alternately into egg yolk mixture. Do not overblend as batter will shrink.

Either with a pastry bag or large spoon, make even lines of batter 4 in. long by 1-1½ in. (10 x 2-3 cm) wide. Sprinkle with a thin layer of powdered sugar. Bake in the middle of oven for about 20 minutes. When lady fingers are done, they should be a very pale brown underneath the sugar coating, slightly crusty outside but tender and dry inside. Remove from baking sheets with a spatula. Cool on cake rack.

Makes about 3 dozen lady fingers.

GERMAN APPLE CAKE

5 apples
6 tbsp. (90 mL) sugar
2 tbsp. (30 mL) cinnamon

Pare, core and slice apples. Sprinkle with sugar and cinnamon. Set aside while preparing the batter.

Batter

3 cups (750 mL) unsifted flour
1½ tsp. (7 mL) baking soda
1½ tsp. (7 mL) baking powder
2 cups (500 mL) sugar
1 tsp. (5 mL) salt
4 eggs
⅔ cup (160 mL) vegetable oil
⅔ cup (160 mL) sour cream
1 tsp. (5 mL) vanilla
⅓ cup (80 mL) orange juice

Preheat oven to 350°F. (180°C).

Add sugar and eggs to oil, sour cream, vanilla and orange juice. Mix well. Add dry ingredients to creamed mixture a little at a time until well blended. Grease a tube or Bundt pan and fill with alternating layers of batter and apples. Sprinkle top of cake batter with additional sugar and cinnamon.

Bake for 1½ hours. Cool 20 minutes before unmoulding, then glaze if desired.

Delicious when served with ice cream or whipped cream.

Makes 8 servings.

Glaze

>   3 tbsp. (45 mL) butter
>   3 tbsp. (45 mL) light brown sugar
>   3 tbsp. (45 mL) sugar
>   3 tbsp. (45 mL) whipping cream
>   ¼ tsp. (1 mL) vanilla

Combine all ingredients in a heavy saucepan and bring to boil over medium heat. Let boil 1 minute. Spoon or pour over cake.

APPLE FANTASIA FLAMBÉ

    1 tbsp. (15 mL) butter
    ½ cup (125 mL) brown sugar
    ¼ cup (65 mL) raisins
    ½ cup (125 mL) brandy
    1 cup (250 mL) apple sauce
    1 tsp. (5 mL) cinnamon
    1 cup (250 mL) milk
    4 eggs
 1½ tsp. (7 mL) sugar
    2 bread slices (buttered on both sides)
      nutmeg to taste

Preheat oven to 400°F. (200°C).

Soak raisins in ¼ cup (65 mL) brandy for 1 hour.

Melt butter in ovenproof dish and sprinkle brown sugar evenly over bottom of dish in the butter. Place in oven for 10 to 15 minutes until sugar caramelizes. Spread apple sauce and raisins, including brandy, over the sugar and sprinkle with cinnamon.

Cut bread diagonally and arrange in dish.

Beat milk, eggs, sugar and nutmeg and pour over bread. Cook in 325°F. (160°C) oven for 50 minutes.

Invert onto serving dish, pour remaining brandy over and flambé. May be served hot or cold with ice cream and whipped cream.

Makes 4 servings.

CANADIAN SUNSHINE

12 peach halves
¼ cup (65 mL) brandy
9 egg yolks
½ cup (125 mL) sugar
¼ tsp. (1 mL) salt
½ cup (125 mL) rye whisky
½ tsp. (2 mL) lemon rind, grated
2 cups (500 mL) whipping cream
3 tbsp. (45 mL) icing sugar
   Meringue Shells (See recipe p. 116)
½ cup (125 mL) toasted almonds, chopped

Marinate peaches in brandy for 1 hour.

Combine egg yolks, sugar, salt, whisky and lemon rind. Cook in double-boiler, beating constantly until very thick. Cool. Combine cream and icing sugar and whip until stiff. Fold into egg mixture.

Fill prepared meringue shells with egg yolk mixture and top with marinated peach half. Sprinkle with chopped almonds.

Makes 12 servings.

MERINGUE SHELLS

- 9 egg whites
- · dash cream of tartar
- 2 cups (500 mL) of sugar

Preheat oven to 270°F. (140°C).

Beat egg whites and cream of tartar until soft peaks form. Add sugar gradually, beating well after each addition. Continue beating until stiff and glossy.

Pipe or spoon meringue onto baking pan covered with foil or heavy brown paper, forming shells approximately 3 in. (7 cm) in diameter. If using a spoon, make a hollow in centre of meringue with back of spoon.

Bake meringues until set (approximately 1 hour). Turn off oven leaving meringues to dry until oven is cool. Leftover meringues may be stored in an airtight container for future use.

Makes 12 meringues.

PEACH DELIGHT

8 egg yolks
12 peach halves — fresh or canned
¼ cup (65 mL) apricot brandy
2 cups (500 mL) whipping cream
½ cup (125 mL) granulated sugar
1 cup (250 mL) dry Marsala
¼ cup (65 mL) brandy

Dice peaches and marinate in apricot brandy. Whip cream and fold into marinated peaches.

Place egg yolks in a medium bowl, add sugar, whip to a lemon colour, add Marsala and brandy. Beat in a double-boiler to a stiff peak. (Curdling occurs if overheated.) Gently fold into the cream and peach mixture. Scoop mixture into champagne glasses and serve immediately.

Makes 8 to 12 servings.

ALMOND SOUFFLÉ

- 1 tbsp. (15 mL) sugar
- 3 tbsp. (45 mL) flour
- ¾ cup (175 mL) milk
- ⅓ cup (80 mL) sugar
- 4 egg yolks
- 2 tbsp. (30 mL) butter
- 1 tbsp. (15 mL) vanilla extract
- ½ tsp. (2 mL) almond extract
- ½ cup (125 mL) toasted almonds, finely ground
- 5 egg whites
  pinch salt
- ¼ tsp. (1 mL) cream of tartar
- 1 tbsp. (15 mL) sugar

Preheat oven to 325°F. (160°C). Toast almonds with skins on for 10 minutes. Grind in blender. Raise oven temperature to 400°F. (200°C).

Butter a 6-cup (1.5 L) soufflé mold. Dust with 1 tbsp. (15 mL) sugar. Tap out excess. In a large saucepan, mix flour with ⅓ cup (80 mL) sugar and milk. Cook over moderate heat until mixture reaches boil. Boil for 30 seconds, stirring constantly. Remove from heat and beat well. Gradually add egg yolks to mixture by adding a little of the hot sauce to the beaten egg yolks and then adding the warm yolk mixture to the sauce. Add 2 tbsp. (30 mL) butter and flavourings. Cover sauce while cooling, to prevent a skin forming.

In a separate bowl, beat egg whites, cream of tartar and salt until soft peaks form. Gradually add 1 tbsp. (15 mL) sugar and beat to stiff peaks. When ready to assemble the soufflé, add almonds to the custard base and gently fold in egg whites. Do not overmix. Pour mixture into prepared soufflé dish. There should be at least 1½ inches (3.5 cm) left between top of soufflé and rim of dish. If necessary, make a collar of several layers of greased foil or waxed paper to extend depth of dish. Place in centre of oven and reduce heat to 375°F. (190°C). Bake 35 to 40 minutes or until a knife inserted in the centre comes out clean.

Serve immediately.

Makes 6 to 8 servings.

GRAND MARNIER CAKE

12 eggs, separated
½ cup (125 mL) all-purpose flour
½ cup (125 mL) granulated sugar
1 tbsp. (15 mL) baking powder
2½ tbsp. (37 mL) Grand Marnier

Filling

2 cups (500 mL) half & half cream
½ cup (125 mL) sugar
5 tbsp. (75 mL) flour
2 eggs
2½ tbsp. (37 mL) Grand Marnier
1 tsp. (5 mL) vanilla
   pinch salt

Preheat oven to 500°F. (260°C).

Beat egg yolks at medium speed for 2 minutes, add sugar; beat for 5 minutes. Blend 5 tbsp. (75 mL) flour into mixture and set aside.

Beat egg whites until peaks hold. Slowly add to yolk mixture and add the remaining flour and baking powder. Blend together gently with hand beater, for approximately 2 minutes, add Grand Marnier. Pour into an ungreased, lined 8 in. x 12 in. x 2 in. (20 x 27 x 5 cm) baking dish. Place cake in oven and reduce heat to 250°F. (120°C). Bake for 45 minutes. When done, cool, slice into two layers. Place bottom layer on serving dish, top with cream filling, place other layer on top. Sprinkle with icing sugar, cut into slices, serve.

Filling

Place 1¼ cups (315 mL) half & half cream, sugar, vanilla, salt in a small pot. Bring to a boil. Beat eggs in remaining ¾ cup (175 mL) of half & half cream for one minute. Add flour, beat until smooth, add slowly to boiling cream. Stir and cook for 5 minutes until thick. Remove from heat, blend in Grand Marnier. Cool. Fill cake.

Makes 10 servings.

ZABAGLIONE (OR SABAYON)

8 eggs, separated
½ tsp. (2 mL) cream of tartar
½ cup (125 mL) sugar
½ tsp. (2 mL) vanilla extract
1 cup (250 mL) Madeira or Marsala
   assorted fresh fruits

In a medium bowl, beat egg whites and cream of tartar with mixer on high speed until soft peaks form. Gradually add ¼ cup (65 mL) sugar, beating until stiff peaks form; set aside.

In the top of a double-boiler, mix together egg yolks, remaining sugar, and vanilla. Place over simmering water and beat with mixer on high speed until thickened and lemon-coloured. Gradually add Marsala. Continue beating over simmering water until mixture mounds when dropped from a spoon, 10 to 12 minutes. Fold egg yolk mixture into beaten egg whites.

Serve immediately over fresh fruit in stemmed glasses.

Makes 8 to 10 servings.

GATEAU AUX ANGES

12 egg whites (room temperature)
½ tsp. (2 mL) salt
1 cup (250 mL) sifted cake flour
1½ tsp. (7 mL) cream of tartar
1 tsp. (5 mL) almond extract
1 cup (250 mL) granulated sugar

Preheat oven to 325°F. (160°).

Sift flour 5 times. Using a large mixing bowl, beat 12 egg whites and ½ tsp. (2 mL) salt on high speed of mixer for 30 seconds. Add cream of tartar and beat until very frothy but not dry.

Gradually add 1 cup sifted flour and 1 tsp. (5 mL) almond extract. Using wire whisk fold in sugar gently but thoroughly. Bake in ungreased tube pan for 45 to 50 minutes until golden brown.

MAPLE MOUSSE

- 1 cup (250 mL) maple syrup
- 1 3 oz. pkg. (84 g) gelatin
- ½ cup (125 mL) cold water
- ½ tsp. (2 mL) salt
- 1-2 tbsp. (15-30 mL) brandy or Grand Marnier
- 4 eggs, separated
- 1 cup (250 mL) whipping cream

Dissolve gelatin in cold water. Bring maple syrup to a boil and simmer 2-3 minutes. Add to gelatin mixture along with salt and 4 egg yolks. Chill in refrigerator until a soft gelatin forms. Beat egg whites until stiff. In a separate bowl, beat cream until stiff. Fold cream, egg whites and liqueur into soft gelatin. Pour into serving bowl and chill until set. This is delicious served with Brandy Sauce.

For Brandy Sauce recipe see page 184.

Makes 4 servings.

ROYAL CANADIAN MAPLE PARFAIT

⅔ cup (160 mL) maple syrup, heated
4 eggs, lightly beaten
1 cup (250 mL) heavy cream, whipped into
   stiff peaks
¼ tsp. (1 mL) salt

Pour the hot maple syrup in a fine stream onto the lightly beaten eggs, beating briskly and constantly. Pour the mixture into the top of a double-boiler and stirring constantly, cook over simmering water until the mixture coats the spoon. Cool, then add the whipped heavy cream and salt. Freeze about 2½ hours in a mold and let set. Cover the chilled mold with lid and/or foil paper.

To unmold, soak a towel in warm water, and wring out. Remove lid or foil from mold, put a serving plate on top and invert mold and plate together. Wrap the warm towel around the mold for a few seconds. Remove the towel and lift the mold to free the ice cream without spoiling its shape. If the surface melts slightly, smooth with the flat of a knife and refreeze the parfait for a few minutes. Top with maple syrup as desired.

Makes 4 servings.

INDIVIDUAL PINEAPPLE SOUFFLÉ MINCEUR

2 tbsp. (30 mL) butter, melted
4 egg yolks
¾ cup (175 mL) drained, unsweetened, crushed pineapple
1 tbsp. (15 mL) pineapple juice
1 tbsp. (15 mL) lemon juice
¼ cup (65 mL) sugar
12 egg whites
dash salt
icing sugar

Preheat oven to 425°F. (220°C).

Lightly butter 12 individual soufflé molds. Mix together butter, egg yolks, pineapple, pineapple juice, lemon juice and sugar.

Beat egg whites and salt until stiff peaks form. (For best results warm egg whites to room temperature before beating.) Gently fold egg whites into pineapple mixture. Spoon into molds. Lower heat to 375°F. (190°C) and bake 10 to 12 minutes. Sprinkle with icing sugar and serve immediately.

Makes 12 servings.

SALZBURGER NOCKERLN

10 egg whites
½ cup (125 mL) sugar
6 egg yolks, slightly beaten
¼ cup (65 mL) flour
⅛ tsp. (0.5 mL) vanilla
    custard sauce (see recipe below)
    icing sugar

Preheat oven to 475°F. (240°C)

Beat egg whites until foamy. Gradually add sugar, beating until stiff peaks form. Carefully fold in egg yolks, flour and vanilla. Spoon into 8 portions on buttered baking pan that has been sprinkled lightly with sugar. Bake 6 to 7 minutes. Remove from oven and sprinkle with icing sugar.

Place on dessert plate and serve with warm custard sauce.

Custard Sauce

1 cup (250 mL) milk
2 tbsp. (30 mL) sugar
4 egg yolks
1 tsp. (5 mL) cornstarch
2-3 tbsp. (30-45 mL) Grand Marnier
2 tbsp. (30 mL) whipped cream

Heat milk and sugar in medium saucepan and bring to a boil. Beat egg yolks and cornstarch until well blended. Gradually add one half of milk and sugar mixture stirring constantly. Pour this mixture back into saucepan. Continue to heat until thickened, stirring constantly. Add Grand Marnier and whipped cream.

Serve warm.

Makes 8 servings.

WESTERN LEMON CLOUD

  1 3 oz. (84 g) pkg. lemon jelly powder
  ½ cup (125 mL) boiling water
  4 eggs, separated
  ⅔ cup (160 mL) sugar
    juice of 1 lemon
    rind of 1 lemon, grated
    whipping cream
    1 lemon, thinly sliced

Mix jelly powder with water and cool until mixture starts to set.

Beat egg whites until foamy. Gradually beat in ⅓ cup (80 mL) sugar, continuing until stiff peaks form. Beat yolks and remaining ⅓ cup (80 mL) sugar until foamy. Add juice and rind. Fold into jelly mixture along with the egg whites.

Spoon into serving dishes and chill for 2 to 3 hours. Just before serving, garnish with whipped cream and thin slices of lemon.

Makes 6 servings.

SOUFFLÉ OMELETTE

2 eggs
1 tsp. (5 mL) sugar
2 tsp. (10 mL) cold water
½ oz. (14 g) butter

Separate eggs. Heat pan over low heat. Beat yolks, water and sugar together until pale and creamy. Fold whites into yolk mixture. Melt butter in omelette pan over moderate heat, pour in the omelette mixture and level. Cook until top is set and bottom is golden brown. Place under broiler for 30 seconds.

Fold, slide onto a warm plate, dust the top with icing sugar and serve at once.

Makes 1 serving.

Suggestions for fillings:

Add one of the following to the cooked omelette:
— 2 tbsp. (30 mL) warmed ginger or orange marmalade
— 2 tbsp. (30 mL) warmed jam
— 2 tbsp. (30 mL) warmed fruit purée
— 1 tbsp. (15 mL) warmed honey mixed with 1 oz. (28 g) chopped walnuts
— 1 tsp. (5 mL) lemon juice and a little grated lemon rind
— 2 oz. (56 g) sliced strawberries soaked in 1 tbsp. (15 mL) Kirsch
— 2 oz. (56 g) whole raspberries

PINEAPPLE PARADISE

½ cup (125 mL) sugar
1 large fresh pineapple
3 eggs
2 oz. (60 mL) sherry or Kirsch
1 cup (250 mL) whipping cream
½ pint (250 mL) fresh strawberries

Slice bottom of pineapple and hollow out. Finely chop pulp. Drain the hollowed-out pineapple in a colander and reserve ½ cup (125 mL) of juice.

In a stainless steel bowl, beat eggs, sugar, sherry and pineapple juice. Bring to a boil and remove from heat. Refrigerate until cool.

Fold the whipped cream into the pineapple pieces.

Pour into hollowed out pineapple and freeze. Put in refrigerator for ½ hour before serving. To serve, cut pineapple into 6 slices and garnish with fresh strawberries.

Makes 6 servings.

KEY LIME PIE

1   10 oz. (280 g) can sweetened condensed milk
¾   cup (175 mL) lime juice
1   tsp. (5 mL) lime rind, grated
3   egg yolks
    green food colouring

Prepare baked graham wafer crust (see Mocha Swirl Cheesecake page 80.) After blending all ingredients, pour into baked pie shell.

Meringue

3   egg whites, beaten
¾   cup (175 mL) white sugar
    pinch cream of tartar

Beat egg whites until stiff but not dry. Add sugar and cream of tartar and continue to beat for 30 seconds. Spread evenly over pie.
Makes 6 servings.

LEMON SQUARES

2¼ cups (565 mL) flour
1 cup (250 mL) butter
½ cup (125 mL) icing sugar
4 eggs
1½ cups (375 mL) sugar
1 tsp. (5 mL) baking powder
1 tbsp. (15 mL) grated lemon rind
5 tbsp. (75 mL) lemon juice
pinch of salt

Preheat oven to 350°F. (180°C). Grease a 9 in. x 13 in. (23 x 33 cm) baking pan.

Prepare crust by combining 2 cups (500 mL) of flour, icing sugar and butter. Press evenly into prepared pan. Bake 20 to 25 minutes.

Meanwhile beat rest of ingredients together. Pour over crust and bake 25 to 30 minutes more or until golden, and lemon custard is set (when tested with toothpick). Dust with icing sugar. Cool in pan on rack. Cut while warm.

Makes 24 squares.

CARAMEL CUSTARD

Caramel

> 6 tbsp. (90 mL) sugar
> 3 tbsp. (45 mL) water

Custard

> 4 eggs
> 3 tbsp. (45 mL) sugar
> 2 cups (500 mL) milk
> vanilla extract

Preheat oven to 325°F. (160°C).

Put sugar and water in a heavy pan and dissolve without boiling. When dissolved, bring the syrup to boiling point and boil until golden brown. Pour the caramel into individual ramekins. Make sure the bases are evenly covered. When cool, butter sides of ramekins.

Blend together eggs and sugar. Warm the milk, then pour into mixture. Mix well and add a few drops of vanilla extract. Strain the custard into the ramekins. Place ramekins in pan half filled with hot water. Bake for 1 hour or until a knife inserted in the centre comes out clean.

Leave the custards in the refrigerator overnight before turning them out on a flat serving dish.

Makes 6 servings.

ITALIAN EASTER BREAD

½ cup (125 mL) warm water
1 tsp. (5 mL) sugar
1 pkg. or 1 tbsp. (15 mL) fast rising active dry yeast
½ cup (125 mL) milk
2 tbsp. (30 mL) margarine
¼ cup (65 mL) sugar
1 tsp. (5 mL) salt
2 eggs, beaten
2¾-3¼ cups (675-815 mL) unsifted all-purpose flour
½ cup (125 mL) mixed candied fruits or raisins
¼ cup (65 mL) blanched almonds, chopped
½ tsp. (2 mL) anise seeds
melted butter
5 coloured uncooked eggs

Frosting

1 cup (250 mL) confectioners' sugar
1 tbsp. (15 mL) milk
½ tsp. (2 mL) vanilla
coloured sprinkles

Preheat oven to 350°F. (180°C).

Measure ½ cup (125 mL) warm water into a large bowl. Stir in 1 tsp. (5 mL) sugar and active dry yeast. Let stand 10 minutes, then stir well. Meantime, combine milk and butter in a saucepan. Heat over low heat until liquid is warm and butter melts. Stir in ¼ cup (65 mL) sugar and salt. Add liquid to dissolved yeast. Add eggs and 1¼ (315 mL) cup flour. Beat until smooth. Stir in an additional 1¾ cups (425 mL) (approx.) flour to make a soft dough. Turn out onto lightly floured board; knead until smooth and elastic, about 8 to 10 minutes. Knead in fruits, blanched almonds and anise seeds. Place in greased bowl, turning to grease top. Cover; let rise in warm place, until doubled in bulk, about 1 hour.

Punch dough down; turn out onto lightly floured board. Divide in half. Roll each piece of dough into 24-in. (54 cm) rope. Twist ropes together loosely and form into a ring on a greased baking sheet. Brush with melted butter. Place coloured uncooked eggs into spaces in the twist. Cover; let rise in warm place until doubled in bulk, about 1 hour.

Bake about 30 to 35 minutes, or until done. Remove from baking sheet and cool on wire rack.

Frosting

Combine frosting ingredients. When bread is cool, carefully drizzle frosting over twist and between eggs. Decorate with coloured sprinkles. Bread may be frozen and decorated after frosting. Remove coloured eggs before freezing.

Makes 8 servings.

See insert for a photograph of this dish.

HARVEY WALLBANGER PIE

1 envelope unflavoured gelatin
½ cup (125 mL) sugar
¼ tsp. (1 mL) salt
½ cup (125 mL) orange juice
¼ cup (65 mL) water
3 eggs, separated
¼ cup (65 mL) sugar
1 cup (250 mL) whipping cream
2 tsp. (10 mL) lemon juice
⅓ cup (80 mL) Galliano or Neapolitan liqueur
2 tbsp. (30 mL) vodka
1 9-in. (23 cm) pastry shell, baked and cooled
2 orange slices

In medium saucepan, combine unflavoured gelatin, ½ cup (125 mL) sugar, and salt. Add orange juice, water, lemon juice, and slightly beaten egg yolks; mix well. Cook and stir over medium heat until gelatin dissolves and mixture is slightly thickened. Remove from heat; cool slightly. Stir in liqueur and vodka. Chill to partially set. Beat egg whites until soft peaks form. Gradually add the remaining ¼ cup (65 mL) sugar, beating to stiff peaks. Fold into partially set gelatin. Whip cream to soft peaks; fold into gelatin mixture. Chill mixture until it mounds when dropped from a spoon. Turn into cooled pastry shell. Chill until firm — 4 to 5 hours. To garnish, make cut in each orange slice from centre to peel; twist and interlock. Place over pie.
Makes 8 servings.

AFTER THEATRE

SHRIMP QUICHE

1 9-in. (23 cm) deep pie shell
4 eggs
1½ cups (375 mL) light cream or evaporated milk
¾ tsp. (3.5 mL) salt
½ tsp. (2.5 mL) pepper
1 tsp. (5 mL) tarragon
1 cup (250 mL) cooked shrimp or crabmeat
½ cup (125 mL) cheese, shredded
¼ cup (65 mL) green pepper and onion, chopped

Preheat oven to 400°F. (200°C). Partially bake pie shell on lowest rack in oven for 8 minutes. Remove from oven and reduce heat to 350°F. (180°C).

Lightly beat eggs, add cream, salt, pepper and desired seasonings. Spread shrimp, cheese, green pepper and onion in partially baked shell. Pour in egg mixture. Bake at 350°F. (180°C) for 35 to 40 minutes or until a knife inserted near the centre comes out clean. Serve hot.

Makes 4 to 6 servings.

See insert for a photograph of this dish.

SMOKED SALMON TART

1 unbaked 9-in. (23 cm) pastry shell
1 egg white, lightly beaten
½ lb. (250 g) smoked salmon, chopped*
1 cup (250 mL) grated Swiss cheese
4 eggs
1¼ (315 mL) cups half & half cream
1 tbsp. (15 mL) fresh dill, finely snipped OR
1 tsp. (5 mL) dried dillweed
½ tsp. (2 mL) salt
¼ tsp. (1 mL) freshly ground pepper
red caviar (optional)

Preheat oven to 400°F. (200°C).

Brush pastry shell lightly with egg white and bake for 5 minutes. Let cool slightly.

Set oven at 450°F. (230°C).

Distribute salmon over bottom of pastry and sprinkle with cheese. Beat all remaining ingredients together except garnish and pour over cheese. Bake 15 minutes. Reduce oven temperature to 350°F. (180°C) and continue baking until top is golden, about 15 minutes. Garnish with caviar if available.

*Use ends and trimmings of salmon if available, as they are less costly.

Makes 6-8 servings.

GREEK SPINACH TARTS

18 medium pastry-lined tart tins
 4 eggs
½ cup (125 mL) plain yoghurt
½ cup (125 mL) milk
½ tsp. (2 mL) salt
¼ tsp. (1 mL) dry mustard
½ tsp. (2 mL) tarragon
   dash nutmeg
10 oz. (280 g) pkg. spinach, chopped, cooked
   and drained
½ cup (125 mL) crumbled Feta cheese

Preheat oven to 375°F. (190°C).

Beat eggs until blended and mix in yoghurt, milk, salt, mustard, tarragon, nutmeg, spinach and Feta. Spoon into pastry-lined tart tins.

Bake for 25 minutes, until set.

Makes 18 quiche tarts.

FRITTATA MISTA

10 oz. (280 g) sausage or diced cooked ham
2 tbsp. (30 mL) butter
2 medium zucchini, about 1½ cups (375 mL) sliced
½ cup (125 mL) medium fresh red sweet pepper (or pimento), chopped
2 green onions, finely sliced
8 eggs
¼ cup (65 mL) half & half cream
2 tsp. (10 mL) lemon juice
2 tbsp. (30 mL) chopped parsley
1 tsp. (5 mL) prepared mustard
½ tsp. (2 mL) salt
1 tbsp. (15 mL) oil
¾ cup (190 mL) shredded Mozzarella

Slice sausages into ¼-in. (0.8 cm) rounds or dice the ham. Slice fresh zucchini into rounds ¼ in. (0.8 cm) thick. Melt 1 tbsp. (15 mL) butter in frypan, sauté zucchini, red pepper and green onion until tender. Remove from pan and set aside. Sauté sausage rounds. Add cream, lemon juice, mustard and salt to the eggs, beating until well blended. Preheat broiler. Place oil and remaining tbsp. (15 mL) butter into 10 in. (25 cm) frypan over medium-high heat. Add mixture to pan, stir in sausage, vegetables and cheese. Scramble until eggs start to set, but are still quite moist. Level surface of mixture. Place under broiler until completely set and puffed, about 2-3 minutes.

Remove from oven and cut in wedges.

Makes 6 servings.

FLAMING GOLDEN OMELETTE

8 eggs
¼ cup (65 mL) soft butter
½ cup (125 mL) table cream
4 apples, peeled and diced
5 tbsp. (75 mL) Calvados or brandy
½ cup (125 mL) castor sugar or fruit sugar
    pinch of salt
    additional sugar

Heat 2 tbsp. (30 mL) butter, add diced apples and brown. Sprinkle with 3 tbsp. (45 mL) of Calvados or brandy. Mix well over a high heat using a wooden spoon, ignite. Add the cream, stir a few minutes over a high heat, reduce heat and leave on simmer.

Break and separate 2 eggs. Add six remaining eggs to the yolks. Add ½ cup (125 mL) of castor sugar and beat lightly with a fork. Add a pinch of salt to the two whites and beat until stiff. Gently fold into previous mixture without beating. Heat a metal serving dish. Heat remainder of butter in pan. Add the beaten eggs. Let cook over a low heat. When the edge begins to turn golden, add the apple preparation to the centre. Fold.

Place omelette on hot serving dish. Sprinkle lightly with additional sugar — about 1 tbsp. (15 mL).

Heat balance of Calvados or brandy slowly. Place serving dish on chafing dish. Sprinkle omelette with hot brandy. Light and serve immediately.

Make 4 servings.

OMELETTE FLAMBÉ MARIE ANTOINETTE

1 pint (1 L) raspberries
1 oz. (30 mL) Kirsch
5 eggs, separated
¾ cup (175 mL) sugar
1 tbsp. (15 mL) icing sugar
2 tbsp. (30 mL) rum, heated

Preheat oven to 425°F. (220°C).

Marinate raspberries in Kirsch.

Beat yolks with ¼ cup (65 mL) sugar until light and creamy. Beat egg whites until foamy. Gradually add ½ cup (125 mL) sugar and continue beating until stiff peaks form. Fold whites into egg yolks. Place ⅓ of the mixture in a jelly roll pan, shaping into oval. Top with marinated raspberries and cover with remainder of mixture.

Bake 8 to 10 minutes.

Sprinkle with icing sugar. Light heated rum and pour over dessert.

Serve immediately.

Makes 4 to 6 servings.

RUSSIAN OMELETTE

2 tbsp. (30 mL) butter
3 eggs
    dash salt
    dash pepper
3 tbsp. (45 mL) salmon caviar
¼ cup (65 mL) sour cream
3 tbsp. (45 mL) water

In a small omelette pan or skillet, melt butter over medium heat. While butter is melting, beat eggs, salt and pepper in a small bowl with a fork or wire whisk.

When cooked, stuff and roll crêpes with the egg and ham mixture and place in a lightly buttered casserole or oven-proof dish. Refrigerate until ready to serve. Bake crêpes for about 10 minutes until lightly browned and bubbly. Serve at once, topped with Hollandaise sauce. (See page 175.)

plate. Spoon sour cream over the top. Garnish with 1 tbsp. (15 mL) of caviar.

Makes 1 omelette.

GOLDEN EGG CRÊPES

Crêpes

>   3 eggs
>   1 cup (250 mL) milk
>   1 cup (250 mL) soda water or beer
>   ½ tsp. (2 mL) salt
>   3 tbsp. (45 mL) salad oil
>   1½ cups (375 mL) unsifted all-purpose flour
>   about ½ cup (125 mL) additional milk or
>   soda water

In a bowl, combine flour and salt. Add eggs one at a time, beating to produce smooth batter. Add salad oil, milk, soda water or beer and continue beating until smooth. Cover and let stand for 30 minutes to 1 hour. After a trial crêpe has been made, add the additional milk or water needed to produce a batter with the consistency of cream.

To make crêpes, heat a 6- or 7-inch (15-17 cm) crêpe pan, and rub with a paper towel that has been dipped in salad oil. Repeat between crêpes. Use a ¼ cup (65 mL) measure for dipping up batter. Pour into crêpe pan, tilting the pan so the batter is coated evenly. Turn with a spatula or pancake turner. Crêpes should be thin and golden brown on both sides. Stack on a plate until ready to fill.

Filling

>   12 eggs, separated
>   ⅔ cup (160 mL) milk
>   2 oz. (56 g) Parmesan cheese
>   4 slices of finely chopped ham
>   ¼ cup (65 mL) unsalted butter, melted
>   salt and pepper to taste
>   additional butter

Preheat oven to 425°F. (220°C).

Beat egg yolks, milk, cheese, salt and pepper until light and fluffy. Add chopped ham and melted butter. Whip 12 egg whites separately until they form soft peaks, and fold into egg yolk mixture. Cook slowly in a double boiler, stirring continuously with a wooden spoon. When cooked, the eggs should be removed from heat. Stir in an additional 3 tbsp. (45 mL) of unsalted butter and allow to cool.

When cooked, stuff and roll crêpes with the egg and ham mixture and place in a lightly buttered casserole or oven-proof dish. Refrigerate until ready to serve. Bake crêpes for about 10 minutes until lightly browned and bubbly. Serve at once, topped with Hollandaise sauce. (See page 175.)

Makes 8 servings.

See insert for a photograph of this dish.

STRAWBERRY OMELETTE

- 4 eggs, separated
- 3 tbsp. (45 mL) icing sugar
- 2 tsp. (10 mL) cornstarch
- 2 tsp. (10 mL) water
- 2 tbsp. (30 mL) butter
- 1 cup (250 mL) fresh strawberries, sliced OR 1 10 oz. (280 g) pkg. frozen strawberries, drained
- 2 tsp. (10 mL) lemon juice

Beat egg whites until soft peaks form, add 1 tbsp. (15 mL) icing sugar and continue beating until stiff. Beat egg yolks with 2 tsp. (10 mL) water and cornstarch until thick and lemon coloured. Fold egg yolks into egg whites. Heat the butter in two small skillets or frying pans, pour in each half of the egg mixture, cook over low heat covered for 5 to 6 minutes.

Divide and arrange the strawberries on one half of each omelette. Fold the fruitless side over and slip onto platter, sprinkle with lemon juice and dust with icing sugar. Serve immediately.

Makes 2 servings.

BAKED DEVILLED EGGS

  3 10-oz. (280 g) cans green asparagus pieces,
     drained
 12 hard-cooked eggs
  6 oz. (168 g) devilled ham
  1 tsp. (5 mL) dry mustard
 ½ tsp. (2 mL) red pepper
  2 tsp. (10 mL) grated onion
  6 tbsp. (90 mL) flour
  6 tbsp. (90 mL) butter
  3 cups (750 mL) half & half cream
  2 cups (500 mL) medium sharp Cheddar
     cheese, grated
  1 tsp. (5 mL) Worcestershire sauce
  1 cup (250 mL) buttered bread crumbs

Preheat oven to 400°F. (220°C).

Butter shallow casserole and place asparagus on bottom. Slice eggs lengthwise and remove yolks. Mash yolks with devilled ham, dry mustard, red pepper and onions. Stuff egg whites with mixture and place on top of asparagus.

To make white sauce, melt butter, stir in flour and gradually add cream. Cook about 5 minutes, stirring constantly. Add cheese and Worcestershire sauce. Stir until melted. Pour over eggs and asparagus. Cover with buttered breadcrumbs and bake for 20 minutes or until brown and bubbly.

May be made the night before and refrigerated, eliminating breadcrumbs, which are placed over top just before baking.

Makes 6 servings.

CHEESE ASPARAGUS ROLL

*1½ lb. (750 g) fresh asparagus
¾ cup (175 mL) sharp Cheddar cheese, grated
¼ cup (65 mL) grated Parmesan cheese
¼ cup (65 mL) bread crumbs
2 tbsp. (30 mL) grated onion
salt to taste, fresh ground pepper
5 eggs, separated
6 tbsp. (90 mL) melted butter

Preheat oven to 375°F. (190°C).
Grease 10 in. x 15 in. (25 x 40 cm) jelly roll pan.
Line with wax paper and grease.

Wash asparagus and cook for 3 minutes. Drain and dry. Chop fine. Combine with cheeses, onion, salt and pepper. Beat in 5 egg yolks. Stir in melted butter.

Beat egg whites until stiff. Fold into asparagus mixture. Pour into prepared pan. Spread evenly and bake for 15 to 18 minutes. Turn out onto clean tea towel. Let stand 10 minutes and then remove wax paper. Cut in half crosswise. Roll up. Cool. Unroll when cool.

*Frozen asparagus may be used. Thaw completely before using.

Filling

>   4 tbsp. (60 mL) butter
>   4 tbsp. (60 mL) flour
>   2 cups (500 mL) of 2% milk
> 1½ tsp. (7 mL) prepared mustard
>   salt and pepper
>   6 hard-cooked eggs, chopped

Melt butter, add flour and milk. Cook over low heat until thickened. Add mustard, eggs, salt and pepper. Spread over asparagus roll. Roll up. Heat in a warm oven before serving.

Makes 6 servings.

SCRAMBLED EGGS EN BRIOCHE

8 eggs
4 large (or 8 small) brioches or patti shells
(available in supermarkets)
2 oz. (60 mL) table cream
2 oz. (60 mL) butter
2 oz. (60 mL) whiskey
salt, pepper

Remove caps from the brioches. Scoop out and keep hot.

Break the eggs into a bowl. Season with salt and pepper. Beat lightly.

Cook in butter in a shallow frying pan, stirring over a low heat. When the eggs are moist, add the cream. Finish cooking. Add the whiskey. Fill brioches, and serve.

Makes 4 servings.

GOURMET EGG LOUIS

Dressing

    1 cup (250 mL) mayonnaise or salad
       dressing
    ¼ cup (65 mL) chili sauce
    1 hard-cooked egg, finely chopped
    2 tbsp. (30 mL) finely chopped ripe olives
    2 tsp. (10 mL) chopped chives
    1 tsp. (5 mL) lemon juice

To prepare dressing, combine mayonnaise or salad dressing, chili sauce, chopped egg, olives, chives, and lemon juice. Mix well and chill.

Salad

    Salad greens (mixture of spinach, iceberg
       and bibb lettuce)
    9 hard-cooked eggs, cut in quarters
    1 avocado, peeled and sliced lengthwise
    2 medium tomatoes, cut in wedges
    ½ tsp. (2 mL) salt

To prepare salad, wash greens and pat dry. Cut or tear greens into pieces of desired size. Place in large bowl; toss. Arrange hard-cooked eggs in centre of bowl on top of greens. Around edge, alternate avocado slices with tomato wedges. Sprinkle well with salt and serve with Gourmet Egg Louis Dressing.

Makes 4 to 6 main dish servings.

DEVILLED EGGS

6 hard-cooked eggs
2 tsp. (10 mL) mayonnaise
2 tsp. (10 mL) heavy cream
⅓ tsp. (2 mL) salt
⅛ tsp. (0.5 mL) dry mustard
⅛ tsp. (0.5 mL) freshly ground pepper
2 tsp. (10 mL) finely chopped green onions or
   chives
2 tsp. (10 mL) finely chopped parsley
   pimento (optional)
   olives (optional)

Peel hard-cooked eggs and slice lengthwise. Remove yolks. Mash the yolks thoroughly with a fork. Add remaining ingredients and blend until smooth. Taste, add more salt if required. Pipe or spoon into egg whites. Cover and refrigerate for an hour for the flavour to mature.

When serving, garnish each egg with parsley sprigs, thin slices of pimento or sliced olives.

For variety of flavour ¼ tsp. (1 mL) dried oregano, chili powder or curry powder may be added to the yolk mixture.

Makes 12 devilled egg halves.

SCOTCH EGGS

8 hard-cooked eggs
1 lb. (500 g) pork sausage meat
1 tsp. (5 mL) each basil, thyme, sage, salt
   and pepper
   seasoned flour for dredging
1 egg, beaten
1½-2 cups (375-500 mL) dry bread crumbs
   oil or lard for deep frying

Peel and dry eggs. Season sausage meat with herbs. Stir in ½ cup (125 mL) bread crumbs. Divide sausage meat into 8 portions and pat out into rounds on a dampened board. Place an egg on each round; fold the sausage meat to envelop the egg so the egg is completely covered. Roll in seasoned flour; brush with beaten egg and coat with remaining crumbs. Allow to dry 10 to 15 minutes. Heat deep fat to 375°F. (190°C). Fry scotch eggs in deep fat until deep golden brown. Cool, cut in half to serve. Serve hot or cold with Creamy Horseradish Sauce; see page 176.

SPINACH APPETIZERS

4 tbsp. (60 mL) butter
3 eggs
1 cup (250 mL) all-purpose flour
1 cup (250 mL) milk
1 tsp. (5 mL) salt
1 tsp. (5 mL) baking powder
1 lb. (500 g) Edam cheese, grated
2 10 oz. (280 g) bags of spinach, rinsed and chopped

Preheat oven to 350°F. (180°C).

Melt the butter in a 9 in. x 13 in. (23 x 33 cm) pan in the oven. Beat eggs well. Add flour, milk, salt, baking powder and grated cheese.

Squeeze as much water from raw spinach as possible. Add to above mixture and blend well. Pour into prepared pan. Bake for 35 minutes. Allow the cooked mixture to stand for approximately 45 minutes before cutting. This dish may be cooked ahead and reheated before serving.

Makes 4 servings.

BAKED EGGS

12 hard-cooked eggs, cut in half
2 cups (500 mL) medium white sauce (see page 178)
1 3 oz. (84 g) pkg. chipped beef
1 tsp. (5 mL) onion, grated
   salt and white pepper to taste
   Parmesan cheese
   paprika

Preheat oven to 350°F. (180°C).

Make a white sauce, adding onion and finely-chopped package of chipped beef. Salt and pepper to taste.

Place eggs in flat baking dish and pour sauce over. Sprinkle generously with Parmesan cheese and enough paprika for colour.

Bake for 20 minutes.

This may be prepared ahead and reheated at 350°F. (180°C) for 10 minutes.

Makes 6 servings.

CHEDDAR CHEESE SOUFFLÉ

6 eggs
1 tbsp. (15 mL) butter, softened
½ cup (125 mL) heavy cream
¼ cup (65 mL) grated Parmesan cheese
½ tsp. (2 mL) prepared mustard
⅓ cup (80 mL) flour
½ tsp. (2 mL) salt
¼ tsp. (1 mL) pepper
½ lb. (250 g) sharp Cheddar cheese
11 oz. (308 g) cream cheese

Preheat oven to 375°F. (190°C).

Butter a 5-cup (1.25 L) soufflé dish or other deep baking dish, or 5 or 6 individual baking dishes.

Place eggs, cream, Parmesan cheese, mustard, flour, salt and pepper in container of electric blender. Whirl until smooth. Cut cheddar cheese into pieces and add, piece by piece, to mixture in container while motor is running. Cut cream cheese into pieces and add to container. When all cheese has been added, whirl mixture at high speed for 5 seconds. Pour soufflé mixture into prepared dish. Bake for 45 minutes for a soft, liquidy centre, or 50 minutes for a firm soufflé. The soft, liquidy centre is particularly delicious, as it serves as a built-in sauce to be spooned over the soufflé. Bake individual soufflés for 15 to 20 minutes. (Top will be golden brown and slightly cracked when baked the maximum time.) Serve immediately.

Makes 6 servings.

See insert for a photograph of this dish.

INDIVIDUAL LOBSTER SOUFFLÉS

3 eggs, separated
1 truffle or mushroom
1 oz. (30 mL) brandy
1 tbsp. (15 mL) whipping cream
1 lb. (500 g) fresh lobster or 1 5½ oz. (154 g) can
    of lobster meat or crab
2 tbsp. (30 mL) butter
2 tbsp. (30 mL) flour
1 cup (250 mL) milk
¼ tsp. (1 mL) dried chives
    pinch cayenne
    salt and pepper to taste

Preheat oven to 375°F. (190°C).

To make roux: melt butter, stir in flour and continue stirring until golden brown. Gradually add milk and brandy, and simmer. Stir in dried chives and simmer for 10 minutes. Add chopped lobster, chopped truffle, cayenne, salt and pepper. Remove sauce from heat. Cool slightly and beat in egg yolks. Beat egg whites until stiff and add whipping cream. Fold into the sauce. Divide mixture evenly between 4 individual buttered soufflé molds and set them in shallow pan of water. Bake the soufflé in moderately hot oven for about 15 to 20 minutes.

Makes 4 servings.

GARDEN CLUB SOUFFLÉ

2 tbsp. (30 mL) butter
2 tbsp. (30 mL) flour
2 cups (500 mL) milk
1 tsp. (5 mL) salt
⅛ tsp. (0.5 mL) cayenne
1 tbsp. (15 mL) grated onion
1 tsp. (5 mL) each of fresh basil, parsley, tarragon or chives
4 eggs, separated

Preheat oven to 350°F. (180°C).

Melt butter, stir in flour, slowly add milk; stir and cook 5 minutes. Cool slightly, add 4 egg yolks, heat until mixture begins to thicken.

Beat 4 egg whites until stiff. Stir 1 tbsp. (15 mL) beaten egg white into soufflé mixture. Fold in the rest.

Turn into unbuttered straight-sided soufflé dish and set in pan of hot water.

Bake until as firm as desired (45 to 60 minutes).

Serve from baking dish.

Makes 4 servings.

CRÊPES WITH HAM & CHEESE SOUFFLÉ

3 tbsp. (45 mL) butter
¼ cup (65 mL) flour
1 cup (250 mL) milk
    salt and pepper
    pinch grated nutmeg
1 tsp. (5 mL) prepared mustard (Dijon)
4 egg yolks
1 cup (250 mL) grated Gruyère cheese
6 oz. (168 g) ham, finely diced
6 egg whites
12 crêpes

Preheat oven to 425°F. (220°C).

Prepare crêpes as per instructions on page 14. Line each cup of a buttered muffin tin with one crêpe.

In a saucepan, melt the butter, whisk in the flour and cook until foamy. Pour in milk all at once and bring sauce to boil, stirring constantly. Season with salt, pepper and nutmeg. Simmer 2 minutes. Remove from heat and beat in mustard and egg yolks. Return to low heat and cook until mixture thickens slightly. Remove from heat and let cool slightly. Stir in grated cheese and ham. This mixture can be prepared 3-4 hours ahead up to this point. Rub the surface of warm mixture with butter to prevent a skin forming, or cover with clear wrap.

Whip the egg whites until stiff peaks form. Warm the cheese mixture and gently fold in egg whites. Line each cup of buttered muffin tin with one crêpe shell.

Fill crêpe shells ⅔ full with soufflé mixture and bake for 6 to 7 minutes until crêpes are browned and soufflé mixture is puffed and set. Serve immediately.

Makes 6 servings.

EGG CROQUETTES

4 hard-cooked eggs, chopped
1 tbsp. (15 mL) butter
1 tbsp. (15 mL) flour
¾ cup (175 mL) milk
1 egg, beaten
½ tsp. (2 mL) salt
   dash paprika
1 tbsp. (15 mL) Romano or Parmesan cheese
12 crackers, crushed

Melt the butter in a saucepan. Blend in the flour, salt and paprika. Heat until mixture bubbles. Remove from heat. Add the milk gradually, stirring constantly. Bring to a boil, stirring constantly, and cook 1 minute longer. Cool slightly and mix in the chopped eggs and cheese. Set aside to cool. When cold, shape into croquettes. Roll in cracker crumbs, dip in egg and roll again in crumbs. Drop into deep fat heated to 375°F. (190°C). Fry until golden brown, about 5 minutes. Remove from fat, drain and serve.

Makes 8 to 10 croquettes.

THE GOLDEN EGG

2 hard-cooked egg yolks
4 uncooked egg yolks
¼ cup (65 mL) white wine (semi-dry)
 dash salt
 dash pepper
8 slices toast
8 slices smoked salmon
8 eggs, poached and kept warm

Put hard-cooked yolks through sieve and set aside.

Beat uncooked egg yolks and wine and season with salt and pepper. Place in top of double-boiler and cook over simmering water, stirring constantly until thickened. Stir in sieved egg yolk. Keep sauce warm.

Place toast on platter. Cover toast with salmon slices. Place poached eggs on top of salmon slices and cover with sauce.

Makes 4 to 8 servings.

EGGS JOSEPHINE

4 eggs
2 English muffins
1 cup (250 mL) Mornay sauce (See page 175.)
¼ cup (65 mL) cooked ham, diced
½ tbsp. (7 mL) Parmesan cheese
1 tbsp. (15 mL) butter

Prepare Mornay sauce and add diced cooked ham. Poach the eggs, arrange in deep baking dish on small slices of toast or toasted English muffins. Pour Mornay sauce over the poached eggs. Sprinkle with Parmesan cheese. Dot cheese with butter. Bake under broiler for 10 minutes or until golden brown. Serve with salad or as an entrée.

Makes 2 to 4 servings.

EGGS COMTESSE

4 poached eggs
1 12 oz. (336 g) can artichoke hearts
1 7-oz. (196 g) can mushroom purée
    Parmesan cheese
1 cup (250 mL) Béchamel sauce (see page 179.)

To poach the eggs, place in saucepan and add enough
water to cover 1 inch above the eggs and bring the
water to just below boiling point. Break eggs one at a
time into saucer or cup and slip gently into water.
Always poach eggs at the simmering point. Sauté 4
artichoke hearts in butter and arrange on a platter.
Heat mushroom purée and garnish the hearts. Top
each with a poached egg and cover with a well-
thickened Béchamel sauce. Sprinkle with Parmesan
cheese. Brown in the oven and serve.

Makes 2 servings.

See insert for a photograph of this dish.

EGG FOO YUNG

Sauce

> ¾ cup (175 mL) chicken stock
> 1 tbsp. (15 mL) soya sauce
> 1 tbsp. (15 mL) cornstarch, dissolved in 2 tbsp. (30 mL) cold water

Bring stock to a boil and add soya sauce and cornstarch mixture. Cook over low heat until thickened. Reheat to serve over omelettes.

Omelettes

> 6 eggs
> 1 tsp. (5 mL) salt
> ½ cup (125 mL) cooked shrimp, pork or chicken, diced
> 1 cup (250 mL) bean sprouts, fresh or canned
> 3-4 mushrooms (about 125 mL), chopped
> ½ cup (125 mL) green onion, finely chopped
> oil as needed

Beat eggs and salt until blended. Add shrimp, mushrooms, bean sprouts and onions.

Heat about 2 tbsp. (30 mL) of oil in moderately hot frying pan. For each omelette, pour about ¼ cup (65 mL) of the egg mixture into the pan. Cook about 1 minute until lightly browned on the bottom, then turn and cook on the other side for another minute. Transfer to a heated serving platter and keep warm.

Repeat with remaining egg mixture, adding oil to the pan as needed.

Makes 4 servings.

DRINKS

MANDARIN NOG

    2 eggs
    2 medium mandarins cut in chunks
    2 scoops vanilla ice cream
    1 cup (250 mL) milk
    ¼ tsp. (1 mL) nutmeg
    2½ oz. (75 mL) rum

Combine all ingredients. Blend until frothy. Pour into tall glasses and serve.
Makes 2 servings.

PINK CLOUD

    2 eggs
    1½ cups (375 mL) chilled cranberry juice
    ¼ cup (65 mL) orange juice
    2 tsp. (10 mL) lemon juice
    2½ oz. (75 mL) vodka or gin

Combine all ingredients. Blend until frothy. Pour into tall glasses and serve.
Makes 2 servings.

EGGNOG

    1 egg, well beaten
    2 tsp. (10 mL) sugar
    1 cup (250 mL) milk or ½ cup (125 mL) light cream
    ¼ tsp. (1 mL) vanilla extract
    nutmeg

Beat together all ingredients, except nutmeg. Pour into tall glass and sprinkle with nutmeg.
Makes 1 serving.

BRANDIED CHOCOLATE EGGNOG

>   2 eggs, separated
>   2 tbsp. (30 mL) cocoa
>   ¼ cup (65 mL) of sugar
>   pinch of salt
>   pinch of cinnamon
>   1¼ cups (315 mL) milk
>   ½ cup (125 mL) whipping cream
>   ½ cup (125 mL) brandy
>   nutmeg

Combine cocoa, 2 tbsp. (30 mL) sugar, salt and cinnamon in small saucepan and mix well. Stir in half of the milk. Cook, stirring constantly, until mixture reaches a full boil. Remove from heat, add remaining milk and chill well.

Shortly before serving, beat egg whites to soft peaks. Gradually beat in remaining sugar, beating to a soft meringue.

Beat cream to soft peaks. Beat egg yolks with brandy; beat into chilled chocolate mixture. Fold meringue and ⅔ of the cream into chocolate base. Pour into tall glasses, top with remaining whipped cream and nutmeg.

Makes 6 cups.

CHRISTMAS EGGNOG

3 egg yolks
¾ cup (175 mL) sugar
¼ tsp. (1 mL) salt
3 cups (750 mL) milk
1 cup (250 mL) heavy cream
1 tbsp. (15 mL) sherry
3 egg whites
  nutmeg

Beat egg yolks; gradually add ½ cup (125 mL) sugar and salt, beating constantly. Gradually add milk and cream. Cook over hot water, stirring constantly, until mixture is thick enough to coat a spoon. Cool. Add sherry; chill. Beat egg whites until stiff; gradually add remaining ¼ cup (65 mL) sugar, beating constantly until stiff. Fold into chilled custard. When ready to serve, pour into chilled punch bowl; sprinkle with nutmeg.

Makes 2 quarts (2 L) or 16 4-oz. (112 g) servings.

SYLLABUB

4 egg whites
2 cups (500 mL) white wine
¼ cup (65 mL) grated lemon rind
⅛ cup (80 mL) lemon juice
1½ cups (375 mL) sugar
3 cups (750 mL) milk
2 cups (500 mL) light cream
nutmeg

Combine wine, lemon rind and lemon juice. Stir in
1 cup (250 mL) sugar and continue stirring until dissolved. Add the milk and cream. Blend until frothy.
Beat the egg whites until very stiff. Add remaining
sugar a little at a time. Put half of the egg whites into
the wine mixture and blend well. Add remaining egg
whites by spoonfuls, allowing to float on top. Put into
glasses or small mugs and sprinkle with nutmeg.
Makes 10 servings.

SAUCES

HOLLANDAISE SAUCE

2 eggs yolks
2 tbsp. (30 mL) white wine
¼ cup (65 mL) clarified butter*
   salt, pepper, juice from ½ lemon

Cream the egg yolks and white wine in a stainless steel saucepan over a low heat. Gradually add the clarified butter, salt, pepper, lemon juice. Keep warm.
   Makes ½ cup (125 mL).
Note: Although not really difficult to make, Hollandaise sauce may separate due to overbeating, adding the fat too quickly, or overheating. To rescue a curdled sauce try one of the following:
— Beat another egg yolk in a small bowl. With a whisk or fork, gradually beat in the curdled hollandaise.
— Place 1 tbsp. (15 mL) water in a small bowl. With a whisk or fork, beat in a small amount of separated sauce until it becomes smooth. Keep adding sauce slowly, while continuing to beat vigorously.

*To clarify butter, melt completely over low heat. Remove from heat; let stand 5 minutes allowing the milk solids to settle to the bottom. Skim the butter fat from the top, and strain the remaining clear yellow liquid into a container.

CREAMY HORSERADISH SAUCE

¾ cup (175 mL) sour cream
3 tbsp. (45 mL) prepared horseradish
1 tbsp. (15 mL) prepared mustard

Blend thoroughly. Chill.
Makes approximately 1 cup (250 mL).

CANADIAN CHEDDAR CHEESE SAUCE

¼ cup (65 mL) butter, melted
3 egg yolks
¼ cup (65 mL) flour
1½ tsp. (7 mL) salt
¼ tsp. (1 mL) white pepper
2 cups (500 mL) hot milk
½ lb. (250 g) Cheddar cheese, grated
¼ tsp. (1 mL) dry mustard
dash paprika

Mix together butter, flour and egg yolks and cook over low heat 8 to 10 minutes. Gradually blend in heated milk and cook until thickened, stirring constantly. Stir in cheese until cheese has melted. Simmer 15 minutes. Add seasonings and strain. Serve with Fried Golden Egg.

Makes approximately 3½ cups (875 mL).

MARCHAND DE VIN SAUCE

⅓ cup (80 mL) minced mushrooms
½ cup (125 mL) minced green onion
½ cup (125 mL) minced onion
½ cup (125 mL) minced ham
1-2 garlic cloves, pressed
½ cup (125 mL) butter
2 tbsp. (30 mL) flour
  pepper and cayenne to taste
¾ cup (175 mL) beef stock
½ cup (125 mL) claret
  salt to taste

Lightly sauté vegetables, garlic and ham in butter until onion is transparent. Stir in flour, pepper and cayenne. Brown mixture lightly, about 10 minutes, stirring constantly. Blend in stock and claret. Salt to taste, cover and simmer 15 minutes over low heat. Stir occasionally. Sauce may be refrigerated for future use.
Makes 1½ cups (375 mL).

MUSTARD SAUCE

½ cup (125 mL) white sugar
2 heaping tbsp. (30 mL) dry mustard
½ cup (125 mL) white vinegar
2 eggs, well beaten
1 tbsp. (15 mL) butter

Cook gently (preferably in a double-boiler) until thick, stirring constantly. Remove from heat and add butter.

Store in refrigerator in covered container.

Makes approximately 1 cup (250 mL).

WHITE SAUCE

4 tbsp. (60 mL) butter
4 tbsp. (60 mL) flour
2 cups (500 mL) milk
salt and pepper to taste

Melt butter in small, heavy pan. Blend in flour and cook for 2 minutes, stirring constantly.

Gradually add milk, stirring well after each addition. Cook until thickened and smooth.

Makes approximately 2½ cups (620 mL).

MORNAY SAUCE

To basic white sauce add:

   ½ cup (125 mL) grated each of Swiss and
       Emmenthal cheese
   2 tbsp. (30 mL) Parmesan cheese
Makes approximately 3 cups (750 mL).

BECHAMEL SAUCE

   Make as basic white sauce. Add 4 beaten eggs to
milk, slowly add to flour and butter mixture and cook
until thickened and smooth.
   Makes approximately 2½ to 3 cups (625-750 mL).

BLENDER HOLLANDAISE SAUCE

   3 egg yolks
   1 tbsp. (15mL) lemon juice
       dash cayenne
       dash salt
   ½ cup (125 mL) butter

   Melt butter until bubbly but not brown. Remove
from heat. Put egg yolks, lemon juice, salt and cayenne
in blender on "high". After 3 seconds, remove lid and
add butter in a slow steady stream and blend for
another 30 seconds or until thick and smooth.
   Serve at once.
   Makes 1 cup (250 mL).

BASIC MAYONNAISE RECIPE

4-5 egg yolks
1 tsp. (5 mL) salt
⅛ tsp. (0.5 mL) cayenne pepper
2 tsp. (10 mL) prepared mustard
2 cups (500 mL) oil
1 tbsp. (15 mL) lemon juice
2 tsp. (10 mL) vinegar

All ingredients should be at room temperature.

In a large bowl, mix egg yolks, salt, cayenne and mustard. Using a blender beat in ½ cup (125 mL) of oil very slowly. When mixture thickens, pour in an additional ½ cup (125 mL) in a slow steady stream. Alternately add remaining cup (250 mL) of oil and the lemon juice.

Should the mixture separate, place 1 yolk in a bowl or blender. Slowly beat mixture into the yolk, beating with a whisk or fork until emulsion is complete.

Makes 2½-3 cups (625-750 mL).

MARVELLOUS MAYONNAISE

1 cup (250 mL) white sugar
2 tbsp. (30 mL) dry mustard
2 tbsp. (30 mL) flour
1 cup (250 mL) white vinegar
6 eggs, beaten
1 8 oz. (224 g) carton sour cream

Mix all ingredients in a double-boiler and cook, stirring until thickened. Remove from heat and add sour cream. Refrigerate.

Makes approximately 3½ cups (875 mL).

BÉARNAISE SAUCE

¼ cup (65 mL) white wine vinegar
¼ cup (65 mL) dry white wine or vermouth
5 tsp. (25 mL) finely chopped green onions or shallots
½ tsp. (2mL) dried tarragon
¼ tsp. (1 mL) dried chervil (optional)
⅛ tsp. (0.5 mL) pepper
3 egg yolks
¾ cup (175 mL) cold butter cut into 6 pieces
minced fresh parsley

In a small saucepan or the top part of a double-boiler, combine the first 6 ingredients. Boil uncovered, stirring occasionally until mixture has reduced to 3 tbsp. (45 mL). Cool to lukewarm.

Remove from heat, beat in the egg yolks with a wire whisk. Set pan over low heat and with the whisk touching the bottom of the pan, beat the mixture until yolks begin to thicken slightly. Quickly remove from the heat and beat in 2 pieces of the butter. Return to low heat and continue beating until smooth. Remove from heat and beat in 2 more pieces of butter. Repeat the beating over low heat, then remove again and add the last of the butter. Whisk and add the parsley.

Serve warm, not hot.

Makes approximately 1 cup (250 mL).

EGG AND CHEESE DIP

   1 8 oz. (224 g) pkg. Cheddar cheese, room
      temperature
   4 hard-cooked eggs, chopped
   1 tbsp. (15 mL) Worcestershire sauce
   2 tbsp. (30 mL) relish
   1 tbsp. (15 mL) mustard
   1 green onion, finely chopped
1-2 tbsp. (15-30 mL) chopped green pepper
   2 tbsp. (30 mL) mayonnaise

Mix well and serve on crackers, or as a raw vegetable dip. Refrigerate covered until serving.
Makes 2 cups (500 mL).

BUTTERSCOTCH CREAM SAUCE

   3 egg yolks
  ¾ cup (175 mL) light cream
  ½ tsp. (2 mL) salt
  ½ cup (125 mL) brown sugar
   1 tbsp. (15 mL) butter
   1 tsp. (5 mL) vanilla

Into top of double-boiler, place egg yolks, cream, salt
and brown sugar. Cook over medium heat until sauce
thickens, stirring constantly. When thickened, remove
from heat and add butter and vanilla.
Makes 1½ cups (375 mL).

VANILLA SAUCE

4 egg yolks
1 cup (250 mL) heavy cream
1 cup (250 mL) milk
½ cup (125 mL) sugar
½ tsp. (2 mL) vanilla

Scald the cream and milk. Beat the egg yolks until light and add the sugar. Combine egg-sugar mixture with the hot milk and cream and cook over boiling water, stirring constantly until it is the consistency of custard. Add vanilla and stir.

Makes approximately 2½ cups (625 mL).

CUSTARD SAUCE

1 cup (250 mL) milk
2 tbsp. (30 mL) sugar
4 egg yolks
1 tsp. (5 mL) cornstarch
¼ cup (65 mL) Grand Marnier
2 tbsp. (30 mL) whipping cream

Heat milk and sugar in medium saucepan and bring to a boil. Beat egg yolks and cornstarch until well blended. Gradually add ½ of the milk and sugar mixture stirring constantly. Pour this mixture back into saucepan. Continue to heat until thickened, stirring constantly. Add Grand Marnier and whipped cream.

Makes approximately 1½ cups (375 mL).

CHOCOLATE CUSTARD SAUCE

2 cups (500 mL) milk or light cream
2 squares unsweetened chocolate
4 egg yolks
¾ cup (175 mL) sugar
⅛ tsp. (0.5 mL) salt
1 tsp. (5 mL) vanilla

In top of double-boiler, heat the cream and chocolate until chocolate is melted. Mix egg yolks, sugar and salt together and slowly add hot chocolate mixture. Return to double-boiler and continue to cook until sauce thickens, approximately 5 minutes. Cool and add vanilla.

Makes approximately 3 cups (750 mL).

BRANDY SAUCE

1 cup (250 mL) sugar
1 cup (250 mL) boiling water
brandy to taste

Place sugar in heavy skillet over low heat. Stir constantly until sugar melts. Slowly add boiling water. Add brandy to flavour.

Chill to serve.

Makes 2 cups (500 mL).

List of Recipes

BASICS

BRUNCH

DINNER

DESSERTS

AFTER THEATRE

DRINKS

SAUCES